Failure Is Unacceptable

Move on to Success

By: Dr. John McElhaney

Your ISBN:
978-0-359-79101-9
Imprint: Independently published

All scripture references are from the KJV

This book is dedicated to my cousin, Ted Hughes, who overcame all the obstacle's and is living his dream.

Contents

Chapter One

Seven words of success

Successful people are not born with a special gene that causes them to become successful, they are also not successful because of who their parents are. Successful people are those people who refuse to allow others or themselves to keep them from pursuing their dreams. Success is an attitude of the mind that must be present if you ever become successful.

The first thing we must do is define success. Success is not measured by money, but most successful people are blessed with a sufficient amount of money. If success is measured by money, then there are a lot of evil thugs that are successful by destroying the lives of others. Success is not measured by fame, some of the most miserable, hateful and disgusting people are famous. Success is not something that makes one proud and arrogant, there are many proud and arrogant people who have no success. Pride pulls you down it does not build you up, pride destroys, humility builds up. What is success then? Success is doing what you love to do every day and being fulfilled because you are living your dream. Doing what you love and loving what you do, when you can make a living this way you will never work a day in your life.

1. The first word for success is Attitude

Attitude must be the number one thing if you are to be successful, according to your attitude so goes your life. Your attitude will determine whether you are a winner or loser. You must learn how to control your attitude if you ever expect to go anywhere in this world. A person with the right attitude, regardless of his surrounding, family, education, money, or circumstances will be successful, he cannot be anything else. A right Attitude drives you to success. Those with the right attitude achieve when everyone around them don't. A person with a right attitude can be in a place where everyone else are losers and he will be a winner. Why? because it is all about how you think, and as you think so are you. You will see everything from the positive not the negative, just like the old saying, "when the world gives you lemons make lemonade", because in the mind of a winner every obstacle is an opportunity. In the mind of a winner every roadblock is a positive thing that is a training experience, I must find a way around, under, threw, or over it. Or, it could be something that would be a turning point that turns you toward something else better than what you are pursuing. Attitude keeps you on track and keeps you doing what you need to do to be a winner. You never win without the proper attitude.

2. The second word for success is Integrity

Integrity, there are a lot of people with money, fame, and power, but they do not have any integrity. You will never be truly successful unless you have integrity. What does the word mean to you, you must first have the right definition for the word? Integrity: the quality of being honest and having strong moral principles; moral uprightness; two of the synonyms are, honesty and honor. A person without integrity will go toward what will give him the most money, fame, or power regardless of whether it is honest or honorable, he will only be thinking of himself and how he can get what will make him stand out in the crowd, regardless of who he must hurt or destroy in the process. A person with integrity wants the best for others as well as himself, he is willing to help others on their way to success, not use them to further his own agenda. You must be aware that everyone that offers to help you on your way are not legit, they are smooth and very persuasive, but their motives are not pure, be looking out for them, and always be skeptical of everyone until you know for sure who they are.

A person with integrity does not ever lie to get ahead, he never defrauds anyone to make a profit, he never tries to get people to work as cheap as he can to farther his profit. His honesty will carry him through when others fall by the wayside.

3. The Third word for success is fortitude

Fortitude; This is a very important word that you need to have in your vocabulary. This word is the word for a person who has the strength of mind to encounter danger, bear pain or adversity with courage. There will be times on your road to success that will be dangerous and painful, but you must be able to handle it with courage. You must be a person who sees everything that happens to you as having a purpose, to help get you to where you want to be. Nothing is easy, that's why most people will never achieve to their potential, they are looking for something easy.

These are the people who buy all the, get rich quick books, and never use them, play the lottery, expect someone else to take them to where they want to be, but are not willing to continue going when the pain gets great. You are not a failure because you fail, everyone will fail many times in life, but you are a failure because you quit and refuse to try again and again and again until you succeed. Look at Thomas Edison, he tried 10,000 times to invent the light bulb before he was successful, what if he had quit on 9,999? then someone else would have gotten credit for the invention and their name would be known around the world.

4. The forth word for success is Resilience

Resilience, the capacity to recover quickly from difficulties; toughness. This is not the same thing as fortitude, although it does go along with it. To be resilient is to be able to bounce back into shape quickly when you are knocked down, this is seen in Thomas Edison very clearly, else how could he try 10,000 ways to invent the light bulb. If you are not willing to get back up and keep going when you have faced a defeat, then you will never know success. This also has to do with attitude, that is why I said from the beginning that attitude is key, without the right attitude you can forget success, Resilience, has to do with how we think, knowing who we are, understanding our purpose, and who guides our life.

5. The fifth word for success is enthusiasm

Enthusiasm, great excitement for or interest in a subject or cause. You will never become a success unless you are excited about what you are wanting to do. The excitement alone will drive you when nothing else will. What causes the excitement? The excitement comes because you have a vision of the completion of the thing you are attempting to do. What it will produce when completed. Nothing will drive people like the excitement of being able to perform a task that benefits them. Have you ever seen the excitement in the eyes of a child when they going to Disney World, or somewhere like that? Or the excitement of seeing something they want and anticipating the dad or mom buying it for them. The excitement of a couple preparing for their wedding day. The excitement of grandparents over the birth of a grandchild. If you are not enthusiastic you will never know true success.

6. The sixth word for success is perseverance

Perseverance continued steady belief or efforts, withstanding discouragement or difficulty; persistence. Here is another word that relates well with the other words we have chosen. These words all must be present if you are going to be successful. When you look at the winners against the losers, you see those who are winners are those who refuse to give up, you can't stop them, they keep going and going and going, just like the energizing bunny. Losers drop out before the task is finished because of some difficulty, but the winners don't allow the difficulty to stop them, it is just something to help them discover another way to overcome the obstacles, Winners and losers are measured by what it takes to stop them. One of the greatest things you could do for yourself is to watch the ants as they work, they never quit, they always find a way around whatever is in their way, they will move the largest object to get the job done and they always are willing to help another ant with his load. Leaf cutter Ants are a species of ant that cut the leaves off trees, a colony of these ants can remove every leaf off a large tree in one night. Why, because of perseverance.

7. The seventh word for success is humility

Humility, this word does not sound like a word you would want if you are striving for success, but that is because people do not understand what humility is. Humility is not weakness, cowardice, inferiority or unconcern, but humility is power under control. Like a horse that has been broken to ride, or work. The horse hasn't lost any of his strength or ability, but now he is useful and can be used for many good things. A person with out humility is like a horse that has not been broken, his showing off his power is not helpful but destructive. You will never know true success without humility. A humble person is a person who does not feel superior to anyone else, he puts others above himself, realizes who he is and where he would be in life without God. A humble person will always treat his employees with respect and pay them well. He will not be in business to get rich himself off the backs of others but will be interested in the employee's welfare as well. This is another thing that comes from a right attitude. Humility is

something that when you think you have it you just lost it. Humility is not to think little of yourself but to not think of your self at all. One of the biggest problems we have is with pride, you can trace this back to every problem we have in our life. Pride, believing I am somebody special and others are less than me, I am smarter, wiser, stronger, prettier, better at what I do, superior to most other people. Pride just raises its head all time, we must always be aware of that because nothing is as destructive as pride.

Attitude, Integrity, Fortitude, Resilience, Enthusiasm, Perseverance, Humility, keep these words in your mind, learn the definition of each one so you will be able to use them when the time comes.

Chapter Two

Attitude is the key

Never underestimate the power of a right attitude. I am sure all of you have been around people with a bad attitude, when everything they say is negative, nothing is right with anything in the world or with their life. They complain about everything and everyone. This kind of people destroy everyone around them, the worse kind of people you can have working for you are negative people. When you have someone like that among the work force, production goes down, you have more people who miss days of work, you have more injuries, you have more sloppy work and if you don't get the persons attitude changed then you have to get rid of them because they are just like one rotten potato in a bag of potatoes, the bad potato will cause the whole bag to go bad just in a little while.

Now it also works in reverse, you have a person with a great positive attitude and the opposite is true. A positive person among the work force will increase production, people will miss less work, there will be less sick folk, less injuries, and a happier work place with a lot less stress. Stress is one thing that causes more health problems than anything and stress is certainly connected with negative attitudes. Therefore, management is always looking for positive people with a great attitude to hire. If you want to get haired on a job, go in with a great positive attitude. If you get up each morning with the right attitude you will accomplish much more that day than you could ever have thought. The people around you will be friendlier, the birds will sing louder and prettier, the trees and flowers will look so much prettier, and the work you do that day will not seem like a chore at all but a joy to be involved in it. The reason I know this is because I have experienced it. I have done a lot of things in my life, things that turned out good and were a joy to do I did with a positive attitude, but the things that did not turn out good at all and caused me more grief that anything else I can lay the blame on a bad attitude.

There are many of you reading this right now know that I am telling you the truth. Let me ask you to do this before you go on reading this book. Stop and think about the things you have screwed up in life and things that turned out to be a disaster, and I bet if you analyze the situation properly you will see clearly that your attitude was to blame.

You get a right attitude by how you think, you must begin thinking positive about everything. Even things that look like there is nothing positive about it. The bible is our guide book for life and it says in I Thessalonians 5:18, In everything give thanks: This means we are to live thankful for everything everyday regardless of how it looks to us. Also verse 16 of this same chapter says, rejoice evermore, which means we are to live in a state of rejoicing always. Having a right attitude is refusing to allow the negative thoughts to stay in your mind. You can't keep them from springing up, but you must replace them as soon as they do spring up with positive thoughts. It's like one man said, "you may not be able to stop a bird from lighting in your hair, but you don't have to let him build a nest there." It is up to you to change your thinking.

How to get a positive attitude. There are some ways that will help you become more positive in your thinking.

Begin looking at the positive side of everything. From looking at your job from the prospective of, "Man, I must go to work today" to, Wow, I get to go back to work today", this will cause you to look at your work as a positive thing and you will be able to relate to all the positive aspects of the work. What can I learn new today from my job, what positive input can I receive today from my co-workers, I am going to do my job so well today that my manager will be so pleased, I wonder if there will be someone at work today that needs an encouraging word that I can give them. As you go through your day with this attitude you will be surprised at how much better you feel, how much better everyone else acts, how much better you enjoy the work you do, and the whole work experience will be a positive experience that even affects your attitude when you get home. I know some of you are saying, "that is easer said than done", not if you realize what makes this possible. Your thoughts come from what you put in your mind. So, the next thing that will help you become more positive is.

Read and fill your mind with positive things; One of the best ways to program your mind to be more positive is to read and the books you read need to be books that will build you up not tear you down. The best books to read to put you on the road to success is first the bible, I don't know how much you read of the bible, but I would recommend you read it every day. You will be surprised how much you will be affected by getting a good picture of who God really is, when you see God for who he really is then you will see your self for who you really are, and the bible will guide you as to how to deal with this. Man's greatest problem is that he needs to be brought back into a right relationship with Holy God and only when this happens can you know what real success is.

The next kind of books to read are biographies or autobiographies of men who have been an influence on the world in a positive way. You will find out that all these men had one thing in common and that is a strong belief in God. Look at the difference in men like William Wilberforce, men of the reformation like, Martin Luther, John Knox, John Calvin, men like Jonathon Edwards, and then contrast them with men like Stalin, Hitler and Mussolini, and other Atheist and you will see the vast difference in those who have a strong belief in God and those who don't.

Another kind of biographies to read are books of those who have started successful businesses, there are many on the market. One great book you might want to read is, "Start Small Finish Big", by Fred DeLuca, the man who started the Subway restaurants. I would also recommend you read, "Gifted Hands", by, Dr. Ben Carson. Some of the greatest motivating, inspiring and positive speeches, by one of the greatest speakers of all time are the speeches given by Dr. Martin Luther King, Jr, I have all his speeches and I love to listen to them. The lesson you need to learn is, put only positive things in your mind. The bible tells us this, Paul when he was writing the letter to the church in Philippi, said this in **Philippians 4:8, *Finally, brethren, whatsoever things are true, whatsoever things are honest, whatsoever things are just, whatsoever*** *things are pure, whatsoever things are lovely, whatsoever things are of good report; if there be any virtue, and if there be any praise, think on these things.*

Another good book to read is, "Defending the Free Market", by; The Rev. Robert Sirico, this is one of the best books on the free market that I have seen.

The third thing you can do to become more positive in your thinking is to surround yourself with positive people. There is a saying that tells us how we can determine the type mind a person has by what they talk about. Small minds talk about people, medium minds talk about current events, great minds talk about ideas. Watch and listen to people when they speak, what are they talking about. If they want to gossip about other people all time you are dealing with small minded people, they will never help you grow but will keep you down. If they talk about current events, they are not too bad we need to discuss this at times, but they will never take you far. If they are always talking about some new idea they have then stick with these people because they will wind up going places. Always surround yourself with great minds and those who are always encouraging you. I can tell you right now from experience and you already know this as well, most people are going to discourage you more than they will encourage you. You cannot share your dreams with most other people, they are only going to tell you why you cannot do that. Just look at those who are telling you why you cannot do something, and notice, they have never done anything, why would you listen to them.

Continue to reprogram your mind from negative to positive and you will be surprised at how your thinking will change, you will wake up one day and realize, you don't look at things as you once did, you always change the atmosphere in a room and people are excited to be around you. When you look at people you will see them in a different light, from where and what they are to where and what they could be if they only made the right decisions. People with the right attitude will be encouragers not discouragers. They will always tell you how you can live out your dreams and to dream big. This is the way you will act when you have developed a right attitude. You will always be encouraging everyone around you.

Another thing that will keep your attitude right is to get enough rest. There is nothing good about burning the candle at both ends, it only wastes the candle and does not light any other room. Our bodies are made for rest. That is why God, said, "six days shall you labor but on the seventh day you shall rest." Not just man but the animals that are used for work. We also have day and night. The day for working and the night for sleeping. If you are going to be a positive person, you are going to have to properly take care of your body. Leave off things that are harmful to your body, like, tobacco, drugs, alcohol, overeating, and overworking. One of the things that entrepreneurial persons do more than anything else is over work, and not properly take care of their body, because they are driven from the desire on the inside to be successful, they many times neglect to eat and sleep properly, not because they are partying or doing something like that, but they can't seem to stop working, their mind is always developing new ideas etc.

One of the things that I recommend highly is for families to take vacations often. If you are a person with a drive for success you need to, stop get your family and go somewhere you can enjoy each other for a week or two every so often. Do not take your work with you. This is going to be hard, but you and your family need this time. I always say, there are two things I have used money for that I never regret. One is the money I give to the church, my tithes. The other is what I have spent on vacation for my family. I have always gotten more back from this than what I gave. Do not neglect your family, no job, business, or anything is more important than your family. If your child has a ball game, involved in something at school, recital, etc. always be there, do not let anything get in your way. Never neglect your wife or husband, you will never get back what you lose by not being there for your spouse and children. You will never regret being available for your family. A successful person is a person with a happy family.

Chapter Three

Learn everything you can

A lot of people do not care anything about learning. If you look at the school system today it is just about impossible for teachers to teach the students because so many of them are not interested in learning and don't want anyone else to learn. They disrupt the class until it is impossible to keep order much less teach. So, what you have are the students who really are positive minded and have a desire to learn, they learn despite what is going on. This you must know. If you can learn, (and what I mean by that is, unless you have a mental disability that makes it impossible for you to learn) you can learn and there is no excuse for you not learning. If you can read, you can educate yourself, most of the learning that you will do in life will be through your own efforts and because you have a desire to know things. So, get this straight, every person that wants to learn can and will learn to the level that they desire, regardless.

Learning is done through many methods. Reading is one of the best ways to learn, but you can't get everything you need by reading. Another way to learn is by observing others that are doing something that you might want to do. Another way is listening to those who know what they are talking about. Practicing what you would like to do. Let's take these one at a time.

Reading: If you are not a reader then begin, because I do not believe you will ever know true success unless you are a reader. There is so much you can learn just through reading. I have thousands of books in my library, I always have some reference I can go to when I need insight on something. When you read you need to focus, let the message sink in so it will be absorbed in your mind, so you can remember it when you need it. There is a verse in the bible in **Romans 12:2 *And be not conformed to this world: but be ye transformed by the renewing of your mind, that ye may prove what is that good, and acceptable, and perfect, will of God.*** This verse lets us know that we need to reprogram our mind from the way it has been programed by the worlds way of thinking to God's way of thinking. Your mind has been programed from the time you are born, to think a certain way. The programing happens by what you allow in your mind, through what you hear, read, see, and practice. Therefore, we all must totally reprogram our thinking if we are going to be people that are winners. There are a few people who have been raised in a positive environment, with parents that have been an inspiration to them and have constantly pushed and encouraged them to be their best at everything they do. Many times, these folks will go on to continue in the profession of the parents and do great at what they do. But, even among those families there are some who never amount to anything because they start thinking wrong and get the wrong attitude. Parents can only do so much, it is up to the individual as to whether he wants to be a success or a bum, and the responsibility lays totally on his shoulders. As I have said before, read biographies, and autobiographies, this will give you an idea of what others did to overcome the obstacles in their life and get to where they wanted to be. You also need to read books that are instructional, these will give you information on what you are interested in doing. I would also recommend you read history, learn all you can about the history of your country as well as the world. You need to be able to continue a conversation with anyone you meet about the things they are interested in. I know that whatever your passion is, will be what you read about the most, that is a good thing, because you need to know everything you can on the subject that interest you the most, because this will be what will drive you as you go on your journey to success. I know some of you may be thinking, "reading, I hate to read," if you will force yourself to read, it won't be long until you can't pass a bookstore without going in. I remember when I was in grade school I would always be reading an encyclopedia, dictionary, or something like that, the teacher would have to tell me to put it down when we were going to start a class. I wanted to know all I could about everything I could from as early as I can remember.

Listening; This is something I have always been interested in all my life, listening to others talk who know more than me, and about everyone will know more about somethings than you do. There is one kind of person who will never go far and never be respected and that is someone that thanks he knows everything and will not listen to anyone. You have seen these kinds of people, you cannot tell them anything, they are a legend in their own mind. There is no use wasting your time with these people, they only upset you. Be willing to listen to what others have to say. When I was a child I would set and listen to the adults talk for hours and be so excited listening to their experiences. When a person knows too much to listen to anyone else, he is headed for a fall. Another way to listen is recordings others have made. I have listened to tens of thousands of recordings of bible teachers and preachers and have always gotten something from them. You can always find a recording of someone speaking on what ever you are interested in. Do not waste time when you are driving, exercising, or resting, be listening to recordings that are instructional. There are books on CD that you can listen too, but I would not let that take the place of reading. I like to read the book rather than listen to the recording, I just seem to get more out of it. When I read I can stop and meditate on what I have read for a while, I also can read a section over if I need too, to help me get the meaning of what is being said. But, if you must listen to the book being read, do it, it is better than not doing it. One of the problems people have with listening is they are always listening to the wrong kind of things. There are things that you do not want to listen too, just like there are books you should not read. Do not listen to filth, this will only corrupt your mind and keep you from thinking properly. Do not listen to gossip, this will only make you think small. Don't listen to the wrong kind of music because music whether you believe it or not is so powerful and it will direct you in a wrong direction before you know it, it is very persuasive, it becomes ingrained in your mind and takes a hold that is hard to remove. If the music is not uplifting and positive leave it alone. If you show me what a person puts in their mind, I can tell you in what direction these people are going and where they will wind up if they do not change.

Observe; When you see others doing what you want to learn this is worth a lot more than you will ever know. You can read about something, listen to people talk about it, but then when you see someone doing it, you will get to see the actual process being done not just talked about. Remember you must do whatever it is that you are enthusiastic about, or it is just a desire. How many people do we know who never achieve anything, because they never were willing to begin? When you are observing, do it until you understand it completely, don't just observe a few minutes and think you are ready, there are things that go wrong that you will not understand until you have observed for a long time. Get all the observation you can.

Practice; We now come to the stage of practicing what you would like to do. How do you do that? You do it by going to work for someone that is doing what you would like to do. It is better to work free for someone to learn the trade than it is to get paid on a job that is not going to give you anything you can use later. Learning a trade from an employer involved in a trade you can learn to do and build a business, is worth much more than you make on a job. Even if you must go to an employer and say, "if you will let me, I will work for you for free for a month, I am interested in the business you are in. Now if it is an employer in the town you are going to start a business in, he may not be so ready to do it, because it will mean he is going to have competition, but hardly anyone would turn down free labor. If you need too, get your self haired on with the employer, and work until you know the business. You can do this as many times as you need too, with as many employers as you need, to learn different kind of trades. I knew a man in Florida, who begin working on different jobs learning different trades, bricklaying, building, landscaping, many different trades. Then he started business in all the different trades. He had five children, that grew up as he builds the businesses. Then then in 2003, for Christmas he gave all five of the children one million dollars each. You never go wrong learning a trade and putting it into practice.

Chapter Four

Refuse to listen to nay Sayers

I cannot emphasize this enough, please do not listen to the negative people around you that are always telling you why you cannot do something. I don't want to discourage you but, most of the people you know including family are going to be quick to tell you why you can't do what you have a burning desire to do. That is why you cannot share your dreams with most people because they will discourage you very fast and very harshly. You will have to keep your dreams to yourself most of the time, unless you find a winner who has a positive mind and is a dreamer of large dreams. If you do find someone you can share your dreams with and they will encourage you to follow your dream that is a wonderful thing. But these folks are hard to find.

What you must do is refuse to allow anyone to discourage you to the point of giving up on your dream. If you look at the men throughout history that have achieved success you will see people that refused to give up even when it seemed hopeless. I would challenge you to read the stories about, Henry Ford, Colonel Sanders, Thomas Edson, Walt Disney, Abraham Lincoln and many others who refused to give up until they achieved what they were pursuing. Colonel Sanders was 62 years old with nothing but a 106.00 social security check. He had come up with a fried chicken recipe when he was in his fifties. He now begins to take this recipe to restaurants trying to get someone to take it and add it to their menu for a royalty, he traveled all over the United States hearing no after no everywhere he went, he slept in his car but kelp going. He got no 1009 times before he got a restaurant to accept his offer and that was in Salt Lake City Utah. 1009 failures but finally a win. The restaurant that took his recipe tripled its sells the first year and 75% of the sells were the colonels chicken. This became the first Kentucky Fried chicken restaurant.

I do not know about you but when I am walking on the treadmill or the track, where I walk, I always go a lot longer than I thought I could. The reason I can do that is because I don't go till I get tired wanting to stop and then say, well I believe I can go another thirty minutes. No, I say I believe I can go another five minutes and I focus on five, sometimes one. The reason a lot of people fail is because they set the goal to far ahead. You don't start out to Miami, from where I live all at one time. You must go through all the towns between before you get there. I start out going to Chattanooga, then to Atlanta, then to Macon, then to Valdosta, then to Gainesville, then to

Orlando, then to Miami. It is a step at a time. Getting to where you want to go in life happens, when you are willing to take each step along the way that will get you there. There are other ways to go to Miami, that will take you a different route, but it takes longer. Are they bad routes? No, sometimes it may be good to take a longer route. You may learn something along the way that would benefit you in the future that you would not learn if you go the fastest route. The key is to get to where you want to go and learn everything you can along the way. The journey is the most exciting part, especially for an entrepreneur.

When Colonel Sanders begin his journey to sell his chicken recipe, if he had known at that time, he would go to 1009 separate places and hear all of them would say no, would he would have started out? Probably not, but he went a step at a time. Each time he got a no, he would say, "Let me try one more time". That is what got him there and that is what will get you to where you want to go. Just about everyone that is successful, if they knew how hard it would be to get there probably would not have attempted it and would have settled for something less than the best. But they started out and did not allow anything or anyone to stop them, they went a little farther, and a little farther, until one day they were there.

Do not settle for less than what your desire is. To do so is to live a mediocre life, never satisfied with where you are. It will affect everything else in your life, your family relationships, friends, coworkers, everyone around you will be affected by the way you act because you are living below what was meant for you.

Getting to where you want to be in life is not easy. When people tell you that it is, they are lying to you. These are the people that want to sell you the get rich quick packages and formulas, that are supposed to show you how you can get rich without doing anything, and the money just begins to accumulate in your bank account. Don't buy into that. Ask yourself this question, "If this formula is so good and produces this much money, why do they want to sell it to me, doesn't selling it to me cut down on what they could make if I take some of the market?" Where they are making their money is off fools like you and me, who want to make money easy and fast with no work. The thing we must understand is that getting rich fast and easy will not satisfy you. It is not the money that satisfies, it is the accomplishing something that you set out to do.

Why do so many people who are second, third or more generations that get large inheritances from their family when someone dies, run through the money, and have no appreciation at all for what they got? The reason is, they did not make the money, it is just money to them, just like winning the lottery, those people act the same way. When you receive large amounts of money through an inheritance, the lottery, or some other way, you only see what the money can buy, there is no joy of knowing that this is money made from my pursuing my dream and with all the hard work that went into it I now see the results.

Having money does not mean you are successful, most rich folks are miserable. Success is being able to enjoy what you have achieved. Successful people do not flaunt their wealth, that's rich people without success. Successful people do not waste their money, by extravagant living, or showing off. They know money is a tool to use. Successful people are more interested in using their money in a positive way that will benefit others and produce more income. Remember, you will have a lot more people that will tell you why you can't do something than you will that will encourage you. You also will have those who will not say anything to discourage you, but really, they don't believe you will accomplish what you desire too. They will tell others that you have some big ideas, but you will get over it and come back to earth when you see those things are not possible. That's why you can only shire your dreams with some people a step at a time.

Chapter Five

Follow your Dream

Dreamers are a different brand of people. They usually don't function well with the rest of society. They are the ones many people, even teachers look at as never being able to learn to the equivalent of others. The reason for that is their mind is focused on other things. Things that are far beyond everything the normal people are focused on. When you look back at some of the most successful people of the past, you will see this is true.

Thomas Edison's teachers told him, "he was too stupid to learn anything." He also was fired from his first two jobs because he was not productive. Later he went on to invent many of the things that were world changing devices like the electric light bulb, the phonograph, the movie camera etc. Edison held over one thousand patens on his inventions. He certainly didn't let what the teachers said stop him, or what his employers thought about him slow him down. He followed his dream. He was so focused on his dream that none of the things others thought about him mattered. He was marching to the sound of another drummer, that he was listening to afar off, and the negative statements others made about him didn't resonate with him.

Dr. Seuss had his first book rejected by twenty-seven different publishers, but later went on to sell over six hundred million books and became known around the world.

Sir James Dyson, went through all his savings and 5,126 prototypes that failed, but the 5,127th worked and he became the number one seller of the bag less vacuum and worth 4.9 billion dollars.

Walt Disney was fired from his job at the newspaper because they said he lacked imagination.

Benjamin Franklin, had to drop out of school at ten years of age, because his parents could no longer afford to send him. He educated himself by reading on his own and we all know what became of him.

Zig Ziglar, failed seventeen times before he succeeded in the speaking business, but now his name is a household word. Almost everyone that is in business has listened to Zigs motivational tapes or have been to where he is speaking. I have used his tapes and been to hear him speak many times. He was a fine Christian man that lived a life that revealed Christ. And his moto was, "you can have anything you want in life as long as you help someone else get what they want in life."

Stephen King's first novel was rejected by 30 publishers. He was so disheartened he threw it into the garbage. His wife took it out had him to finish it, his books now have sold over 360 million copies.

Abraham Lincoln, lost his job, defeated for state legislature, failed in business, sweetheart died, had a nervous breakdown, defeated for speaker, defeated for nomination for congress, elected to congress, lost re-nomination, rejected for land officer, defeated for U.S. senate, defeated for nomination for vice president, again defeated for U.S. senate, then he was elected to the president of the United States.

You must follow your dream and to do so you must stay focused. Your failures must not stop you, but only make you more determined to succeed.

J.K. Rowling had just gotten a divorce with a baby, she was on government welfare and could barely afford to feed her baby. She wrote her first book, shopped it around to dozens of publishers, having to type each copy of the 90,000-word manuscript by hand because she couldn't afford a computer or to get it photocopied. Finally, a small London publisher gave it a chance because the CEOs eight-year-old daughter loved it. Now look at where she is with her Harry Potter series.

Tyler Perry had a rough childhood. He was physically and sexually abused growing up, got kicked out of high school, and tried to commit suicide twice—once as a preteen and again at 22. At 23 he moved to Atlanta and took up odd jobs as he started working on his stage career.

In 1992 he wrote, produced, and starred in his first theater production, I Know I have Been Changed, somewhat informed by his difficult upbringing. Perry put all his savings into the show and it failed miserably; the run lasted just one weekend and only 30 people came to watch. He kept up with the production, working more odd jobs and often slept in his car to get by. Six years later, Perry finally broke through when, on its seventh run, the show became a success. He's since gone on to have an extremely successful career as a director, writer, and actor. In fact, Perry was named Forbes' highest paid man in entertainment in 2011.

"Don't let the negatives of life control you. Rise above them. Use them as your stepping stones to go higher than you ever dreamed possible." – Mary Kay Ash.

Chapter Six:

Surround Yourself with Winners

You cannot surround yourself with losers and expect to be a winner. I know you have heard the old saying, "You can't soar with the eagles, if you waddle around with turkeys." This is what a lot of people try to do. The people you associate with affect you more than you can imagine, that's why you see successful people only surrounding themselves with other successful people.

Winners have a positive outlook on life.

Winners will always have a positive word to say, because you cannot be a winner with a negative attitude. You will always feel build up when you leave talking to a winner. There is just something about a person that is a winner that draws people to them and leaves them feeling good about themselves. The positive attitude does not change with the circumstances if it did they would not be winners. When circumstances get in the way a winner will be contemplating a way to get around, across, or over the circumstance, they never wait for the circumstances to get better before they proceed with their dream. Let this sink into your brain right now because you are going to need this many time on your way to your destiny.

Winners talk about ideas and are not interested in foolishness.

Have you been around people who only talk about foolishness, never anything of substance? Those people are never going anywhere, because their mind is totally useless in producing constructive thoughts. I see these people all time and can't wait to get away from them. What they talk about is an irritation to your ears, like someone scratching a chalkboard with their fingernails. Everyone they associate with are the same way, because like attracts like. And the old saying is correct, "birds of a feather flock together." I know a lot of people thank I am unsociable, or snobbish, but that is not me at all, I'm just a person who wants to discuss things of importance, things you can learn from, not foolishness.

Winners dress impressive.

This is something that I am very particular about. You can call me old school if you want, but I believe this is one of the things that is destroying the success in this nation. I am not talking about making money when I talk about success, although successful people usually make good money. I am talking about people who with their success comes respect, mentors, role models, people of character, people of responsibility, people who can be looked on as heroes. I am not talking about people with lots of money flaunting it around. Drug dealers have loads of money, organized crime families have lots of money, movie stars, entertainers, and many more that sure are not role models, or people of character have all kinds of money. But, even today when you look at the people who I believe are successful people, they care about how they dress. When you look at Lawyers, going to argue before the court, what do they wear? Nice suits. Why? To show respect to the court and to win the case. The jury is going to judge you by your appearance. Why do you think that the most notorious criminal is dressed in a nice suit when he goes to trial? Because people judge you by how you look. You can argue all you want, but at the end of the day, people treat you with more respect and view you as more important by how you dress. This was very important back years ago and we sure have not gotten better since we changed. I know you have the right to wear sagging pants, (I wish you didn't) and I also have the right not to hire you for a job or not allow you in my establishment. When we dress for success we dress in a way it will give us the edge or allow others to view us as important. I was told to dress for success years ago and I believed it then and still believe it today, that you need to dress in a dark blue suit first preference, you could also use dark gray, or black, white or light blue shirts, and 100% silk ties with some red in it. I still use this model today, I believed the ones that told me that then, now I believe it from experience. So, I encourage you to start following this dress code.

Winners conduct themselves appropriate

If you want to be a winner, you must conduct yourself properly. That means you act appropriately and talk appropriately. Always act as though you are in the presence of very important people. Where you are aware of it or not, you are being watched by others all the time, so conduct yourself in a way that no one can say anything bad about you. Another thing is how you speak. People today cannot express themselves without using foul, vulgar language. Don't do that. Nothing turns me off more than a foul mouth person. He has nothing for me and I don't want to be around them. If you intend to be successful keep your speech clean. Another thing I would encourage you to do is learn to speak properly, using proper grammar, etc. One of the problems we have here in Tennessee is our accent, I have had more trouble with that when I have been in other states than anything. People act as if you are a bumbling, backwoods, ignoramus, just because of my accent.

Winners always have something working in their mind.

One of the reasons you might not be able to get a winner's attention is because they usually have something working in their mind all time. That is why winners usually spend a lot of time alone, and are not comfortable in crowds, like social functions. Their mind is on something they are building, and they can't be distracted by small talk. Let me ask you now. What is your mind on? I know right now you are reading this book. But, is this book getting you to think about how you can implement these suggestions into your life and causing you to think about something you want to do? I hope you grasp what I am saying here and begin to realize you must prioritize your time by cutting out those things that are not going to build you up. Many things we do pull us down from where we want to be, so remove them from your life. Watch only positive movies or movies that will teach you something. Read positive material and only books that will teach you something and build you up. If you want to be a winner, you must follow the rules winners follow.

Winners are respectful

Winners are respectful people, when they are anywhere, store, restaurant, etc. watch how respectful they are. People love to serve them or wait on them because they always leave them feeling good about themselves by the complements they make toward them. People who work with the public have a hard way to go many times because of the attitude of the people they must deal with. Winners are always apologetic toward anyone they see being abused by someone else. They are always grateful toward those who wait on them. Winners treat with respect all peoples regardless of who they are.

Winners are charitable

You never see a winner who is not charitable. When they eat in a restaurant they leave a good tip. This is one of my pet peeves. I hate to see people who do not leave good tips when they eat out. Most of the people who are the most demanding leave the smallest tip. The most respectful people toward the servers usually leave the most tip. I have always said, "If you can't leave a good tip for the server, then stay home and eat." The people who serve you in the restaurant usually have children they are trying to raise by themselves. The pay they receive from the restaurant itself is about $2.00 an hour. They must put up with all kinds of arrogant, hateful, demanding people without getting a kind word or a decent tip, so when you go out to eat remember this. I would never leave less than 20% but I sometimes leave 100-200% or more. Another thing I do a lot is pay for someone else meal while I am there. I love to do this.

Chapter Seven

Try

One of the biggest problems people have that keeps them from becoming successful is the fact they will never try. You must be willing to start. You can set around and dream about what you would like to do, you can set around and talk about what you would like to do, but if you are never willing to try, then you never will do anything. Fear is the biggest reason people never try. People are afraid of failure, but how are you ever going to succeed if you never try. What if Edison never tried to invent the light bulb? Failure was all he did, ten thousand times, but each time he tried again and again until he succeeded. Col. Sanders, what if he had never tried? He never would have failed 1009 times and would have remained broke with his $106.00 social security check. There has never been anyone that succeeded that did not fail, but there are thousands of people that never succeeded because they were afraid to fail and would not try, so they remained in the condition they are in the rest of their life. Try, all you can do is fail, but failing does not mean you are a failure. You are a failure because you will not try. So, try and fail if you have too, but just get back up and say well, I know one thing that will not work, so let me try something else.

Now there are those who are only interested in getting rich. I am not talking about those people. They are the ones who spend all their money on lottery tickets or a gambling gimmick believing they can get rich that way. They never get rich, but if one of those people hit the lottery, they are completely bankrupt again within five years. Why? Because people who get money thrust upon them without working for it do not respect it and are not responsible at all. They live for the moment. That is why when you give people money during disasters, like hurricanes, floods, tornadoes, etc. instead of them taking it and using it responsibly, for food, shelter, clothing etc. they take it and buy designer handbags and things like that never thinking about using it for the necessities of life, looking for the government to take care of their needs. No one should ever get anything without working for it. A person who is not willing to work should be left to himself to either find a way to make it or starve. I know many of you right now are saying, that is no way to talk about people. I am writing this book for people who are sincere about becoming successful, not to people who want to get money any way they can and waste what they get, none of those people will ever know success.

We destroy people when we give them something for nothing. The welfare system in this nation has destroyed generations of people. Why do you see signs in the national parks throughout America, saying "Do Not Feed the Bears"? When you feed them, they no longer must go out and hunt their own food, so they become dependent on the feeding and what happens is this. When there is no one to feed them any longer they don't start hunting food on their own again, but they just sat there and starve. This is what has happened to many people in America. They have been taken care of by the government to the point that they are no longer capable of doing for themselves, and just like the animals would starve if they are not supplied with the necessities, but we must start somewhere to end this welfare curse that was started by president Roosevelt. No doubt he thought he was doing a good thing, but the way it was handled caused it to continue to grow into a monster, and that is where we are today.

When I was growing up I never had a thought of getting money without working for it, it would never have entered my mind. Everyone I knew worked, the men, out side the home and the women, inside the home, but they both as well as the children worked in the garden, also raising hogs, chickens, etc. to eat. There was work, to be done and everyone did it. I worked in the hay fields, hauling hay and putting it in the barn, I also cut fence rails with an ax for 40 cents an hour and was glad to get the work. In the spring I picked strawberries for 5 cents a basket, picked beans for 2 cents a pound to make money to buy what I wanted. There was no allowance from my parents, everything my father made was used to feed, cloth, and shelter us. I had to take cold biscuits and potato sandwiches to school for my lunch, because my father could not afford to give me a dime to eat on. The lunch was 10 cents a day and I could not afford that. There were no free lunches, people in that day believed in making their own way, and we got by fine.

Then the government begin to tell people they were poor, and begin to offer people commodities, this was food substances, flour, butter, powered milk, cheese, lard, just the necessities to live on. I begin to see how just getting those food items begin to affect the attitude of some of the people who received them. They begin to get the mindset that the government will come in and take care of us if we don't have what we need, so people begin to get this attitude of total dependence on the government for their livelihood. What you create when you begin showing people you will take care of their needs is a monster, because you are going to have to increase what you give all the time. Needs will become everything others have who do work and make their own way. The people will continue to demand more and more, and the government continues to give more and more until we have what we have today. Welfare state.

We have people today getting a check from the government saying they are disable because they are an alcoholic, drug dependent, nervous in crowds and can't work, etc. These people get enormous checks each month from the government, who take it from the people who work. Then you have the people who have played the government and get a disability check and work 60 hours a week or more and get paid under the table. People have learned how to play the system and they get money from every government program going. People get a check to take care of their sick relative, mom or dad, wife, husband, etc. and the person who is supposed to be sick draws disability and is no sicker than you or me. I have seen it all, and it all started from Roosevelt's welfare plan that was never checked. Is there no shame, people, be better than that? Determine in your mind that you are going to become successful by following your dream. Put any kind of thinking of getting something for nothing completely out of your mind and go forward toward the dream God has put in your heart.

Don't wait any longer start today toward making your dream a reality, do what you must do, put fear out of your mind and just start.

There is another thing that we fear that causes us not to try and that is the fear of success. You may not believe this but there are a lot of people who will not try because they are afraid they will succeed, and they don't think they can handle it. I bet there are some of you reading this book right now that have this fear, you are saying to yourself, I don't want to begin because what if I succeed and I can't handle it? I will certainly be embarrassed by that. Well just set where you are, and you won't have to worry about that because you never will. What you will find out is as you go along, you will become more confident each day, every time you overcome an obstacle you will become stronger and more confident and by the time you are a success that will not ever cross your mind anymore.

One of the ways to tell what you should be doing with your life is to answer this question. If money was no object, what would you do with your life? How ever you answer that question truthfully is usually what you should be doing. I remember when I was young the thing I wanted more than anything and couldn't hardly wait to do it was join the Army. That was my dream from as early as I could remember. When I became eighteen years old I joined the Army, went to Vietnam and experienced the full effects of being in the Army in a War, I loved every minute of the time I was in the war in Vietnam. I have had a lot of dreams during my lifetime and I don't know of a one of them that I haven't seen accomplished up to this point. Although I am getting older I still have more that I am looking forward to accomplishing. Go for it.

I want to be an encourager never a discourager. I want you to know you can live your dream if you believe you can and are willing to do what it takes to get there. No one will hand it to you, probably no one will even encourage you, if any do it will be only a few, but you don't know how one person can affect you by being an encouragement to you. There is a story I heard sometime back. It is a true story, but I will not give any names. There was a young man one-time back years ago who was the son of a women who was considered just a street tramp. No one knew who his father was including him or his mother. He was made fun of by all the other children and even the parents who thought he was not good enough to associate with them or their children. He was very poor and just ran around fending for himself most of the time because of the kind of mother he had. They were having a special meeting at the church in the community with a visiting preacher who was well known. As the people begin to come into the church, low and behold this young man walked in and walked up the aisle toward the front. The visiting preacher who was greeting people saw this boy, went up to greet him and said to him, "hello it is so good to see you tonight at the service and just who's fine boy, are you?" Well everyone just stopped to see what would happen because they all knew that this boy didn't have a father. But then suddenly before the boy could say anything the preacher said, "Oh, I know whose child you are, the resemblance is overwhelming, you are a child of God, and son you go out and live in a way to make your father proud". A big smile came over the boy's face, his face lite up and from that day forward he lived like a different person. That little boy later went on to become governor of the state of Tennessee and served two terms. Be an encourager you never know how it will affect someone.

Chapter Eight

Refuse to quit

One of the things I learned during basic training in the Army was, they would not let you quit. I remember having to get up around four in the morning and run until you thought you were dead. We would run while it was still dark so, we really couldn't tell how far we had run. You would be so tired, breathing like you were dying, chest hurting like you were having a heart attack. But, when one of the drill instructors saw you were getting ready to drop out he would run up beside you and say, "Trooper, you better not drop out of this run, don't you even thank about it. What is wrong with you momma's baby, pick it up, if you fall out of this run you better be dead when you hit the ground, you, sorry piece of crap." Occasionally, someone would still drop out, but when they did the drill instructors would be down in his face really giving him the devil. What I found out that in a few days no one ever dropped out again. What was going on? What they were doing was showing us that we had a lot more in us than we ever thought we had, and when pushed to the fullest we can do what we never thought we could.

This is something you need to learn if you want to be successful. There is no place to give up, no place to quit, so just suck it up and go on. Why was Edison successful, because he refused to quit? Why was Col. Sanders successful, because he refused to quit? Where did WD-40 get its name? the 40 is how many times it took to get it discovered. The reason we have WD-40 today is because the maker refused to quit. He now has a product that is sold in 160 countries and has over 2,000 uses.

"If you are going through hell, keep going." - Winston Churchill

Let's look at it from the time you were born. When you were a baby you begin playing in the floor. At first you would crawl and then you begin to pull up by taking ahold of things and standing. Then you begin to start to walk. What happened when you started to walk? You failed, but you tried again. Then you failed but got up and tried again. You just kept on trying until you could walk with out falling. Why? Because you wanted to walk more than you feared failing. When you want success more than you fear failure, you will refuse to quit.

When everyone is discouraging you refuse to quit. When circumstances are stacked against you, refuse to quit. When friends begin to laugh at your ideas, refuse to quit. When your body begins to shut down refuse to quit. When you even begin thinking you are a fool for believing as you do, refuse to quit. When everything is gone and there is nowhere to turn, refuse to quit. These are the kind of folks that become successful, are you one of them?

"Why are men so great?" some ask, Well

The heights by great men reached and kept

were not attained by sudden flight;

But they, while their companions slept,

Were toiling upward in the night.

We all talk about the great Babe Ruth, the baseball legend with all his homeruns, but did you know that Babe Ruth struck out 1,330 times?

No one is ever defeated until he gives up.

Why do some people give up? Because they see what they are doing now, but not what they are building. Just like the man who went up to a man laying bricks and ask him, "What Are you doing?" He said, "I am laying bricks". He went up to another man laying bricks and asked him, "What are you doing? The man answered, "I am building a beautiful cathedral." What you see as you work will determine whether you will be successful or not.

Marcus Morton ran sixteen times for governor of Massachusetts, the last time he ran he won, by one vote.

Chapter Nine

Put Priorities right

Many times, people will begin on the road to success but never make it because their priorities were not right. Your priorities are seen in what you spend your time on. You don't have to tell anyone where your priorities are, they see them clearly as they watch what you do with your time. People are never too busy for things that are a priority. Watch what people spend their time on and you will see why they will never be successful.

The number one priority should be your relationship with God. If this is not right, you are already off tract and your success in life will not be success at all. **Mark 8:36 For what shall it profit a man, if he shall gain the whole world, and lose his own soul?**

There is nothing that matters if you don't have a relationship with God. This life is very short and living only begins after this life, so if you refuse to receive Jesus Christ as your Lord and savior, nothing you do or accomplish here matters.

The second priority should be your family. Don't ever allow your drive to succeed cause you to neglect your family. When you get to the top alone it is not worth it at all. The whole reason that you want to succeed is, so you will be able to enjoy it with your family. People will tell you the loneliest place on earth is at the top, especially if you get there by yourself. Make sure you are at home every night with your family. Make sure you remember your wife's birthday, anniversary, etc. Make sure you are involved in all your children's activities. Go to all their ballgames, school functions, recitals, etc. You will find out later that these things are way more important than making money. And one mighty important thing, make sure you are in church regularly with your family. The greatest thing you can do for your children is to love their mother.

The third priority should be your business. I know we talk about success and how we must make sure we allow nothing to cause us to quit as though this is the most important, but now we make it the third down in the level of priority. This is very true, because there are more important things than making money, and if you get these priorities out of order, you are not going to have success, the money you make will not satisfy you and will not make up for losing your family, or your soul. Don't ever listen to anyone or read anyone's book that does not set these three priorities in this order. There are other things beyond these three that you will have to set yourself, but do not get these messed up.

We see people all time that have started out well but have gotten their priorities out of order and have fallen by the wayside. There are many things that will distract you if you are not careful. One such thing is wanting to satisfy a craving before time. Remember a craving is not a necessity. When we get those things confused we are going to mess up. When you look out at people who are losers, all you need do is look at the way they live their life and you will know why. They allow their cravings to rule their life and some lust to them becomes a necessity. These are the people who go out to eat in an expensive restaurant when they have bills they can't pay. People who buy named brand clothes when they can't pay the light bill or house rent. People who must have a new car just to show off when the payment is going to put them into a position to not be able to pay other bills. They get credit cards and max them out on thangs that are totally unnecessary. These people wind up having to work two or three jobs, neglecting their family just to have something that nobody cares about. The people you are trying to impress are not impressed, because when you buy a new Chrysler, they go and buy a new Cadillac. Then you go and buy a new Cadillac, and they go and buy a new Mercedes. If you try to go and buy a new Mercedes, they will go and buy a new Bentley. You will have to ignore trying to impress others if you ever become successful. Look at most of the super-rich people and you will see that they are not interested in trying to impress anyone. You may see them driving a 10 or 15-year-old car or truck, because they could care less what the people that you need to impress say. The people who you need to impress to get them to associate with you are people you need to stay as far away from as possible. They will get you nowhere. People who want to flaunt their money, usually don't have any, they just want to make you believe they do. They are phonies. When you try to satisfy cravings before time it will cause you to lose the most important things in your life. The real successful people do not waste money, that is why they are successful.

Wait until you can afford to buy the things you would like to have that are not necessities, that is what successful people do. The stress associated with debts is so damaging, it destroys your health, your marriage, even your business. Stay out of debt, even if you must drive an old car, live in a small trailer, and eat beans. You will be able to enjoy living later.

Legitimate pleasure, the kind that you can enjoy is paid for before you enjoy it. Illegitimate pleasure, the kind that will cost you everything in the end is paid for afterward. Let me compare this to marriage. The real joyful marriage is the marriage where the couple waited until after marriage to enjoy each other sexually. Others who want to enjoy the sex first and then get married usually don't last long. The honeymoon is so much more joyful when you have waited until you are a legitimate married couple to participle. Look at what the Sacred Scriptures say in **Hebrews 13:4**

The fourth; Marriage is honorable in all, and the bed undefiled: but whoremongers and adulterers God will judge.

Live your life according to God's word and you will never go wrong. You may believe you can get by when others didn't get by, but don't be fooled, you will reap what you sow, and nothing you can do will change that. **Galatians 6:7**

7 Be not deceived; God is not mocked: for whatsoever a man soweth, that shall he also reap.

There is a scripture that is very important to learn, it is found in **Proverbs 23:4**

Fifth; Labor not to be rich: cease from thine own wisdom.

Why does the writer say, not to labor to be rich? Because when riches are his goal then he will do what ever is necessary to attain riches, even if it is wrong or abusive, his only driving force is money. The writer also says not to follow your own wisdom. Because human wisdom will lead you in the wrong direction. We must follow God's wisdom; his wisdom will take you to places of blessings and will never fail.

Winners buy things that appreciate, losers buy things that depreciate. Watch the people who buy the finest most expensive car, when you drive it off the lot it has already lost at least 20 % of its value and will continue to lose more value every day. These people may always be driving the best car, but all their money is gone, and they have nothing that has any monetary value left. The winner buys a car that will get him to where he needs to go for a small amount of money, then he takes what he could be paying on car payments and buys some real property that is going to go up in value. While the loser works night and day just to make his car payment, boat, motorcycle payment and will have nothing worth anything when it is paid, the winner will have paid his real property off and now will have something worth more than what he paid for it in the beginning. He can now use the real property as leverage to buy more and it won't be long until he is worth a whole lot of money because he owns something of value. Don't be fooled by the tricks of Satan, he always tempts you through the eyes. When he gets you to look at something and desire it, he has you hooked. People become paupers, because they listen to Satan, and follow their own wisdom. Wanting to satisfy the lust of the flesh is what destroys people. Then people get upset and angry at people who have accumulated wealth because they chose to forgo the lustful things and suffer without them, so they could enjoy life later. Don't blame others for where you are in life, it is your own fault for the way you used what you had to work with.

Chapter Ten

Never get an ego

You will never become successful if you have an ego. Ego is pride, and the sacred scripture tells us that pride goes before a fall, also when scripture was listing the major sins, pride was at the top. Pride is the worse of the worse. It puts yourself above others, it makes you believe you are the greatest, and causes you to portray that to others. Pride was what caused Satan to be cast out of Heaven. Napoleon was very proud, until he thought he could never lose, but he did lose to a very small place that would never have crossed his mind as a threat, that was Waterloo. Pride blinds you to reality, pride, causes you to become reckless, pride, destroys you in the end. Make sure you come down to earth if you want to be successful.

Ego is driven by the lies we tell ourselves. If you are not careful after you have had a considerable success, you will tell yourself that you alone are the cause of your success and when that happens you are headed for a fall. The truth is that you are the lest cause of your success. There are a lot of others who have helped get you to where you are when you become successful. Never forget those who helped you along the way.

God would be the one who should get the glory for your success, because of him you were born, you had the ability to work and perform what you needed to perform to get to where you are. He is the one that placed within you the desire to do what he has designed you to do. He alone has given you the health, the air you breathe, and the things that enable you to live. Without him you would not even be here today. All glory goes to God. When you do not give him praise for your success, you have then become a fool.

Mother deserves thanks for being the one that carried you in her womb for nine months and then birthing you into this world. Without her you would not be here today. Also, I am sure all along the way your mother has worked hard caring for you as you grew into the adult you are today, never disrespect, or disregard your mother in your success. There is nothing on earth as important as a godly mother in rearing children.

Father deserves your thanks and praise for being the one who made it possible for you being here. Also, if he was a real father, I am sure he supported you while you were growing up and encouraged you along the way. There is no person that has more effect on a child growing up than his father. Do not ever disrespect your father.

Teachers influenced you while you were in school. I am sure some more than others, but the ones who did encourage you and helped you learn the things you needed to learn should be thanked for what they did in your life. Many times, there is one teacher that stands out who really made an impression on you that you never can forget. Always, give praise where it is due.

Family members who have always been there to encourage you when no one else would need to be thanked for what they contributed to your success. It may have been an uncle, aunt, cousin, grandparent, etc. Always remember those who in any way gave you encouragement along the way.

Pastors or clergy who have been a positive example in your life need to be thanked. Many times, we forget about those who have contributed to our success because we just take them for granted because of the position they hold.

Friends, who have been there for you in times of difficulty that you have forgotten about. But many times, if it had not been for some friend who gave us a kind word along the way we may have given up.

Enemies also may have been the very ones who gave you the strength to go on when you were about to quit, because all of their scoffing and mocking may have been what it took to get you on track and refuse to quit, because you just wanted to prove to them that you could do it. Many times, those who mock us the most are really the ones who contribute the most to our success.

 So, what you see when you look at this is that you had very little to do with your success, probably the least of all.

Ego causes us to overestimate ourselves. We become our own determining factor as to what we are capable of, and many times fail miserably.

Ego causes us to refuse correction, or feedback from others. Always be willing to listen to good advice, especially from those who are older and know more than you do. Experience means a lot, so when someone with more experience than you give you feedback. Take it to heart.

Ego causes you to think you need nothing from anyone, you can do it all by yourself.

Ego creates a fool. A person with ego will collapse sooner than later because that is what happens to people who are not willing to listen.

Ego drives people away from you. No one likes to be around a person who is all wrapped up in himself and has all the answers. I try to stay as far away from them as I can.

Ego causes people to fail after an enormous success. The reason for it is the praise a person gets from winning and the desire for even more praise causes them to collapse. The most depressed time in a person's life is right after a big win. Why? Because it is over. What makes a person a success is the joy of the climb, not the reaching the pinnacle itself, but the trip getting there.

I hope you see what I mean when I say that ego is not good, and will look to be humble, because if you do not this world will humble you. **Mike Tyson, said," If you are not humble this world will visit humility upon you",** that is so true

Chapter Eleven

Generosity is a must

One thing you cannot leave out if you are going to be successful and that is generosity. When you look at all the successful people down through history, you will find that they were givers. Giving is just a way of life for successful people. One of the things we learn from the bible is that God blesses those that give and the more you give the more God gives back. You can't out give God. The secret to success is giving not taking. When you see someone, who is looking for every handout he can get, every government program he can take advantage of or every charity he can benefit from, mark that person. He will probably die a pauper never amounting to anything because takers never become successful.

J.C. Penny opened his first store in 1902 and was determined to run it with integrity and never compromise his Christian convictions coming from his three generations of Baptist preachers. He knew that in debt or out of debt his first obligation was to give at lest 10% of everything he made to God. Every Sunday he would give from 10%-30% to the church. Over the years his business grew to over 1600 stores, and his giving continued to increase until he was giving 90% away and keeping 10% for himself.

H.J. Heinz, of Heinz catchup was also a giver, as a Christian he knew that God blesses a cheerful giver. He begins giving 10% and before he died, he was giving 100% of his income to God.

William Colgate, of the Colgate co. was the same as Mr. Heinz, he too was taught to follow God and give his tithe to the Lord. By the time of his death he too was giving 100% of his income to the Lord.

James L. Kraft, of Kraft foods begin giving to God a minimum of 10%. God continued to bless his business until at the time of his death he too, was giving 100% of his income to the Lord.

This goes to show that the more you give the more God will allow you to take in. It is just like a body of water that does not have an outlet. It takes in, but it does not give out. What you have is a pool of stagnated water that nothing can live in, like the Dead Sea. But, if you have a body of water with an outlet, it is always giving out. As more comes in, more goes out and this water is fresh with all kinds of fish living in it. That is the way people are that are givers and non-givers. We are to be conduits not reservoirs.

You can look at the wealthy people of today like Michel Dell, Bill Gates, Warren Buffett and many others and see the multimillions of dollars they give away. Like one man said. No person is successful that dies rich. You think about that.

I personally believe that the Church is to be your first place of giving. Every Sunday you should start out giving a minimum of 10% to the church you attend and as God blesses you increase it. If you are not a giver when you don't have, you will never be a giver when you do have.

Givers are a happy people, they are always looking to bless someone else. Successful people are not self-centered, its not all about them, its about others. The difference between takers and givers is; givers are concerned with helping someone else become successful, takers look at other people only as a means of helping themselves achieve something, never about helping the other person. They use others to get what they want. You will run up on a lot of people during your lifetime that are takers. Many times, you will get taken by them, but the way winners handle that is as a learning experience that will cause them to be more aware of others in the future. You can't help everyone, so don't let it get to you when you find out someone like that. We would like to be able to help everyone, but it is impossible.

There are some people that will always be needy. You could give them a million dollars a year and they would be needed and wanting more. That is why welfare is such a negative thing, because you have a few that will use it as a stepping stone to get out of a desperate situation and move on to a better life. But, then you have those who just take everything they can get and use it, only to become dependent for someone else to take care of. One of the blessings of life is to be raised in a home where there was a work ethic that showed you; if you were to have anything, you work for it, no one owes you anything.

Don't ignore the things I have told you. You might be one of those people who believe you can make it differently than others, and the rules that applied to others don't apply to you. But, just go ahead and try it your way and in a little while come back and tell me how you are doing. I know how you will be doing, not good, because there are somethings that you cannot bypass and become successful.

Chapter Twelve

It takes a lot less time to go from top to bottom than it does to go from bottom to top

There have been a lot of people who worked hard and long to reach the top and just in a little while were back at the bottom. Never believe that you are immune from falling, we are all susceptible to collapsing because of our own stupidity.

I remember a boxer that lived close to me years ago. This man came from the gutter, a trainer saw potential in him and begin working on him to get him to the top. After long hard work he was ready for the title fight of heavy weight champion of the world. He fought heard and won the title. This was a proud day in the life of this man from the gutter. He held a press conference and the news media were there from everywhere. He was recognized by all the magazines and news papers around the world. Everyone wanted to be around him. His next fight came up and he went into that fight strutting around like the top rooster on the farm. Well the bell ring and the fight started. But within the first minute of the first round the great fighter was knocked out, and the fight was over, and his career was over. He never recovered from that fight. All the money he had made from his title fight was spent, he was back on skid row just in a little while. No one cared anything about him anymore, he was homeless again and in just a little while he was dead, and nobody hardly noticed. What happened? He was so caught up in the fame that he forgot about how he got there, and for him to continue to remain at the top he was going to have to keep winning. There were going to be bigger and better men challenging him from now own. How many people have we seen this happen too? Too many to mention.

Don't loose sight of who you are, and don't loose sight of how you got to where you are. Never loose sight of those who helped you along the way, and never fail to give God the glory. When you begin

thinking you have made it, you are a self-made man; then pride begins to rise in you, you are headed for a fall that will wind you up. Remember this world will humble you.

How many corporate CEOs have fallen, and many have even gone to jail because what they really are, comes out when they are tempted. Therefore, you better get this question settled before you ever began on the road to success. If money is what drives you, then eventually it will come out when you are given the opportunity to take a bribe, do something illegal or unethical for money. One of the most important things in your life better be integrity, and it better over rule your desire for money. When money becomes your driving force in your life that over rides everything else, then you are headed for a huge fall. Let me share a story with you.

There was a businessman flying on a plane going to a convention. Seated beside him on the plane was a beautiful married woman. They begin to talk and after a while he thought he would proposition her for a night of sex. He boldly asked her if she would consider spending the night with him for one million dollars, she refused at first but could not get the money off her mind. As the opportunity continued to grow in her mind she kept thinking about what she could do with a million dollars. After a while, after thinking about being so far from home and no one would know about it. It would be only for one night and just think of what she could do for her family with the million dollars. After justifying it in her mind and turning a bad thing into an acceptable thing and then a good beneficial thing she said to the man. "The offer you offered is it still on the table?" He replied, "yes, it is. She said, if it is just for one night I will take it". Then the man said, I need to be honest with you, I don't have a million dollars so how about ten dollars? When she heard that she jumped back and shouted out in anger, "Just what do you think I am?" to which the man replied, "we have already determined what you are, we are now just negotiating a price." What you are will come out when you are put in the right circumstances, so you better have that settled before you ever begin.

There is no shortage of those who have fallen after making it to the top. Tiger Woods, O.J. Simpson, John Edwards, Richard Nixon, Michael Jackson, and many more.

You must always be on guard because Satan, is out to steal, kill, and destroy. He is a lot smarter than you, he knows exactly what will temp you and believe me when I tell you that he will always be around with the bait put out to get you to bite so he can reel you in. Let's look at some of the things that are traps for you to watch for when you are building a business.

Going into business with someone just because you think you need someone, or because you know them and like them. They may be the worse person in the world to be in business with. Not only is it going to hurt your business, but also destroy a friendship. Before you choose a partner for business make sure you need someone. Make sure you know their lifestyle and that they have integrity. Make sure they are interested in the same kind of business practice that you are. Then hire them as an employee first to see if the fit is going to be good. If the fit is not good, then you can remove them with out any problems.

Do not go into debt, just because money is available. Try your best to remain debt free if you can. There are all kinds of money that is available to businesspeople who want to expand, or to have capital on hand, but you do not need to take it. When you see an opportunity to expand on barrowed money, you may be jumping into a trap, that is going to squeeze in on you when the expansion is causing you more to operate and producing less income. Also, if you have extra capital laying around, there is going to be the temptation to spend it on something that you can get by without.

Balance your life. Do not let the company take all your time away from other important things, like family, church, rest, and relaxation. If you build a great business but loose your family, your health, your walk with God or the times you could have enjoyed vacationing with family what benefit is it? Never view success as the most important thing in your life.

Do not be afraid to delegate when it is time. There will be a time when the company will get so big you cannot be involved in everything. When that time comes do not be afraid to allow the people who have worked for you and have proven themselves to you manage some of the load. You will be surprised how good they are at taking responsibility. When we think we are the only one that can keep the company afloat we are headed for a fall. You can only grow to a certain size by yourself.

Do not deceive yourself by believing the company is doing well when it is collapsing. Be ready to make the tough decisions when needed.

Be willing to change when it is necessary. Many people want to be the best at making bulbs for televisions, but televisions do not use bulbs anymore. So, you may be the best that has ever been, but when something is no longer useable making it the best still is nothing. Nothing plus nothing is still nothing.

Be willing to walk away from an idea, or an employee that is failing and costing you time and money. Someone told me one time when I was starting into business that I should never work anyone that takes all my time to work him. I understood perfectly what he was saying, and I have had some of those employees that I have had to get rid of.

Do not hire someone you should not. Sometimes there will be people you know that will come looking for a job. Do not hire them just because you know them, sometimes those people will cause you more aggravation than you can manage. It is easy to begin feeling sorry for someone and give them a job that you should not. I have done it and lived to regret it. Make sure everyone you hire measures up to the qualifications you have for everyone else. You may have someone to get mad at you for a while, but it will save you and your business later.

There are several reasons a business that you start will fail, be aware of the things that cause the failure. Let's look at a few things to be concerned with.

Refusing to get advice. There are proud people who think they know everything and refuse to ask anyone for advice, these people usually wind up failing. Do not be afraid to ask for advice from someone who has already done what you are trying to do. Whether you want to admit it or not, everyone out there knows more about something than you do. So, everyone could teach all of us something.

Expecting wrong results. Many people go into business because they see someone who is in business that is making money and it looks like he does not have to do anything, it just rolls in. So, we get the idea that all I must do is start up this kind of business and set back and reap the profits. What you have not seen is all the time it took the other man getting his business going and all the time he spends keeping it running that you know nothing about. I can assure you if you go into business for yourself, you will work twice as hard as you will be working for someone else.

Starting without experience. If you have no experience in doing what you are planning to do, please wait until you have experience in that field before you begin. If you have too, work for someone who is already in that business, even if you must work for free to get some experience. I can tell you, there are a lot of things you will never learn unless you have worked in that field and working for free to gain experience will be like gold to you in the future.

No accountability. When you go into business you must be accountable for every dime you take in. You cannot run a business like you pick up scrape on the road and take it to the scrap yard, sell it for a few dollars, pocket the money and use it as you want. A business is different from that. There is a lot of overhead. Building rental, utilities, phone, advertising, insurance, bonds, supplies, vehicles, taxes, more taxes, and more taxes, and when you have employees, there is payroll which is your biggest expense. So, every dime you make must be accounted for. When you file your taxes, you will have to account for every dime. Believe me, you do not want the IRS on your back, they never get off.

Trying to live off the business before time.
Some people think they can go into business and it is just like going from one job to another where there is a payroll check that is coming in the next week without fail. No, when you start a business the profit will go back into the business until it is self-supporting and able to support you. I always give this advice to everyone when they ask me about going into business. Do not leave your day job until your business is up and running with sufficient income coming in to pay all expense and pay you a comparable salary.

Treating the business like a hobby instead of a business. Just as there is a danger of trying to live off the business to early, there also is a danger of not leaving your day job and put your full time into running your business when the time comes. Your business will never grow into a real thriving business until you begin treating it as such. Do not be afraid when the time is right to jump into it with both feet, apply yourself and watch your business take off.

Being in the wrong location. There are some businesses that fail simply because they are in a location that will not support that kind of business. Know your surroundings, what is needed and what is not. You would not want to open a snow removing business in Florida, or a surfboard shop in Omaha Nebraska. Check for other similar businesses in the area and see how they are doing before you start yours. Never be afraid of competition, it will only make you become better at what you do.

Failing to respect customers. One thing that will put you out of business fast and that is to mistreat your customers, there will always be somewhere else a person can get what you are selling and believe me they will go there in a hurry if you mistreat them.

Giving up too soon. Many times, a person has given up just before he became successful. It is easy to get tired and burnt out, but do not give up on a project until you are sure it will not work and why it will not work. Study everything you can get your hands on about what you are trying to do. Learn all the ins and outs, the positives and negatives, the methods of running a business of this kind. The profit margins expected from this business.

Not advertising. You may have the best product or service, the best price for what you get, but if nobody knows about it, what benefit is it. People must know about what you have to offer. Your advertising expense will be one of the largest expenses you will have in your business. Look at the expense of advertising on national TV. Companies spend millions every year to advertise their product. And you know what? You keep seeing increased ads for the same product over and over, which means that the companies continue to spend more and more money to advertise their product. Why do they keep doing it? Because it works, if it did not work you would not see the ads anymore. Most advertising is expensive and the more people the ad reaches the more it cost. Your budget will not be able to handle a large amount on advertising at first, so you will have to find out what will give you the best results for your money. Do not be taken in by those selling advertising that is worthless for a large amount. Do some research to find out how to advertise your business.

Find out what others in the same business are doing. If others are using the same kind of advertising over and over and they have been in business for a long time and the business is doing good, then you can be pretty sure the advertising they are using is working. If you do newspaper advertising find out the circulation of the paper. If you do radio, find out how many listeners they have and the radius it covers. For TV use the same as radio. Yellow pages, posters, billboards, handouts, mailouts, signs on autos, T-shirts, caps, and the best advertising of all is word of mouth from satisfied customers.

Test market. You can do this by attaching a discount to the ad, so you will know what is working and how well it is working. If you do a newspaper ad put a coupon with it for a 10-20 percent discount with coupon with an expiration date, so they will act fast. If you do radio or TV, put a discount if they mention the ad.

Do not use false gimmicks to get customers. Make sure that everything you promise a customer you give them. There are so many companies that are unethical when dealing with customers. This always destroys your relationship with good customers that may have been a customer for life. One satisfied customer is worth more than any other kind of advertising. If you promise a twenty percent discount, make sure they get a twenty percent discount. Do not jack the price up forty percent and then discount it twenty, people are not as dumb as you think. Many people will say in advertising, please mention the coupon first. Why? Because if they know you have a coupon, they will jack the price up before they discount it. Do not do that. It would be better to lose money than to deceive someone. You ever notice when there is an auto advertised at a certain price or a certain monthly payment, when you get there that vehicle is always already sold, but they have another that they know you will like at a lot higher price. Always say exactly what you mean and mean exactly what you say, and you will find that the customers will find you. Its never right to do wrong and doing right will always win in the end.

Do not promise something you cannot deliver.
If you are in a service business do not promise
that you will take care of something that you have
no knowledge about or cannot do just to get the
job. What you are doing is creating a lawsuit for
yourself later. People will not see any of the
excellent work you did, only the bad, or
unfinished work you left.

Make sure everything in your ad is correct.
People who hire you from an ad have read the
whole thing, they know what you said, and they
will expect exactly what you have written in the
ad.

Make sure you have a contract. Everything you
are going to do needs to be in writing and signed
by you and the customer. Make sure the price is
established by what is written, because when you
are dealing with contracts only what is written
within the four corners of the contract is binding
and the signatures need to below the writing.
When you are contracting for advertising make
sure everything, they tell you that you are getting
is written in the contract.

Co-op advertising works good sometime. This
is advertising that is done with more that one
business going together and doing an ad together.
It can be in print, mail outs, billboard, circulars,
newspaper, etc. Each business that advertises
pays part of the bill. The more the name of your

business is seen is good, you are getting people to know your business and when they need what you are selling, they will remember you.

Are you getting the idea of what business is and how it works, the things that will keep you afloat and things that will cause you to sink? It will be up to you, as you guide your business on the road to success. You are going to be at the wheel and what happens will be according to you and how you handle it.

Think of your business as a great big ship. The ship is like a large cruse ship weighing some two hundred thousand tons and you are at the wheel. You are having to navigate that big vessel in waters that you know nothing about. You must use your training, wisdom, knowledge and be quick to make decisions. Sometimes you must make decisions that must be made in seconds, so you can't second guess yourself. You must keep it in the deep water, so it will not end up grounded. You must make the right adjustments to the direction, so you will wind up going where you want to go. There is nothing good about getting off course, getting lost and ending up not even close to where you thought you were going. You also must be aware that you are responsible for this massive piece of equipment and if anything happens to it there is no one to blame but you. Think of your business from this analogy and you will be better off. You are fixing to embark on a journey that is going to test every fiber of your being, be strong, stand firm, go forward and never, never, never, give up

Chapter Thirteen

My Story

Let me tell you a little bit about myself. I was born and raised very poor, in the hills of East Tennessee. My childhood was a happy one with the joy of having my father, mother, two brothers and one sister, with one sister dying at birth. I was the oldest and experienced things earlier than my siblings. We were raised very poor, although we did not know we were poor until later in life when the government begin to tell us we were. We had everything we needed, we thought, we didn't miss anything because you don't miss what you have never had.

Our food was the same thing every day, and the same food of everyone I knew. We had gravy and biscuits every morning for breakfast with beans, potatoes, cornbread or biscuits for dinner and supper. Our meat was from the hog you killed in the fall that lasted through the winter. We also had chickens that we would usually kill on Sunday for fried chicken or sometimes chicken and dumplings. We also hunted squirrels and rabbits to eat as well. There would also be fish that we caught and eat. We would pick wild greens to cook that made great eating. Wild berries in the summer for jelly and we canned blackberries for cobbler as well. I plowed with mules when I got about eleven or twelve years old, no one had a tractor. I worked from the time I was old enough to do anything, because I never would have imagined that anyone could receive anything without working for it. Everyone I knew worked and looked forward to working every day. Sunday was church, no one worked on Sunday, it was a day that everyone went to church and come home for a family dinner of fried chicken. Those were good days, the joy of family made it worth it all. Things don't make you happy, money don't make you happy, the things that make you happy cannot be bought.

Some of my first jobs were helping the farmers take up hay in the summertime. We would work in the hot hayfields loading hay on a wagon, taking it to the barn and packing it in the barn loft. You would almost smother to death in that hot barn loft and all the hay dust. I would also help farmers cut fence rails with an ax. Work in the tobacco fields, setting out the plants, suckering and topping the tobacco and then cutting it, hanging it in the barn, then when it is cured stripping the leaves off, grading it, tying it and taking it to market. I also picked beans and strawberries in the spring for two cents a pound for beans and five cents a quart for strawberries. The pay for the hay field, cutting rails, working in tobacco was forty cents an hour. But, the only way you got money when I was growing up was by working. Our parents did not give you money, it took everything they made just for the necessities of living. We got one pair of brogan shoes that cost from a dollar to a dollar fifty. They would look good until you got them wet then the leather would come loose from the soul and you would have to tie the sole on with bailing wire, hog rings, or trout line. I went to school many a day with my sole tied on.

During school I would have to carry my lunch, because I didn't have a dime to eat in the lunch room, it was only ten cents then, but we could not afford that, there were no free lunches in that day and I am glad there wasn't because it may have changed my outlook on life and I would be expecting someone to give me a hand out instead of making my own way. I would take cold potatoes on a biscuit, or cold beans in a jar with a biscuit or cornbread and drink water.

All my life I have had a desire to accomplish things that others did not seem to care about. I wanted to reach above and beyond what others were reaching for and it didn't have anything to do with money, the thrill was in the pursuit. The most exciting time is during the pursuit of building a business or becoming successful. That is why I was always pursuing different things while I was running my other businesses, I never stopped pursuing. And I will have to say that everything I pursued wound up making a profit. I never had a business that didn't make money, some more than others but all made money.

Early in my life I begin selling things. I sold seeds, wall posters, papers, salve, bibles, books, and later in life, insurance, real estate, etc. I worked in sells for companies. If you want to make the most money with a regular job and are willing to do what it takes, you need to go into sells. There you can make what you want too. I have worked on sell jobs for straight commission and made good money, way more than any other job I had working for a company.

I wanted to go into the army from as long as I can remember, so as soon as I was old enough I enlisted in the Army. After my training I was sent to Vietnam where I stayed for one year with God protecting me many times from being killed. After I returned from Vietnam I volunteered to go back three times, but the military would not agree. I was a fugitive fleeing from the FBI until I was captured and sent to prison. That is all I am going to say about that, you need to get my book "When God Will Not Let Go" and read all about what happened in Vietnam and after. You can get that book from Amazon, Barns and Nobel, Xulon press bookstore. Or other places, and if you would like a signed copy, I can send you one.

My First business

My first business that would be considered a genuine business was after I worked for another service company for about eight years as a salesman. As I worked there I was gathering the experience and knowledge of the business so eventually I could start my own business. This is a very good way to get into business. Work for a company and learn the business before you start out on your own.

After I had taken the state exams, gotten my state license, purchased a bond, Insurance and what I needed I then had to quit my job. I certainly could not be working for a company and have a business that was in competition with them. I didn't have a truck, or any equipment to do the work with, but I started a business like that and had to make enough money to live on that first week. Now, I tell you not to start a business this way in the book, but there may be a time when this is all you can do. I got a hold of one of my friends who had started this same business a little while earlier and I ask him if he would service any accounts I sold until I could get my equipment, and he said he would. I also negotiated A real good price, so I would go out sell a treatment, get him to do the work for about fifty percent of the price and I would have fifty percent to apply toward my equipment. Within two weeks I had the money to purchase equipment. I also found a friend of mind that had an almost new truck and was wanting a different kind of truck, so he let me take over the payments on the one truck, leaving it in his name until it was paid off, and he bought the truck he wanted, which a little latter I bought the new truck from him as well. He also came and worked for me for about two years. Now I had everything I needed to do business myself.

How did I get the business I needed to live and buy equipment? I went out and sold it from door to door, remember I had been working selling this same service for another company for eight years, so I just did the same thing I had always done. I used telephone soliciting mostly to set up appointments, this worked best for me. Then when I was at an appointment I would knock the doors of all the houses around that one, and sometimes I would come back with three or four jobs right around the one I had the appointment on. Remember I had no money, no equipment, no truck and no way to advertise. That was a formula for failure right there, but that first year I made more money that I had ever made in my life, over six figures that first year starting with nothing. I kelp that business for twenty years raised my children and had my children working in the business as well. I sold the business after twenty years moved to south Florida and opened two more businesses.

Don't let what you don't have keep you from pursuing your dream, there is a way, you can find it. But, remember it takes work and it takes doing what others are not willing to do to reach what you are reaching for.

During the time I was in this business, I was privileged to be able to do a lot of traveling with my family. Once I allowed my employees to handle the business for me, I was free to do about as I pleased. I would spend many weeks on vacation with my family, we were gone traveling at lest half the time. We also liked to cruise so we did that. I remember we were doing a seven-day cruise about once a month for a while. It was such a great time to develop a great relationship with my family. Most parents work all the time and never have time to spend with their family. Just the time spent with family was worth everything. I was also able to give a lot away to church and others. I remember our bill for eating out would average about six thousand a month. I have eaten in the finest restaurants and what I like today better than anything is good old southern home cooking, I still like that gravy and biscuits for breakfast, beans with biscuits or cornbread with greens and some pork for lunch and dinner, I like all the fried vegetables, well just to be honest, I haver never found a food I can't eat.

What is the best business to go into?

I would have to say a service business is the best business to go into. I have been in different businesses and a service business is the one I would recommend. Look at a few reasons.

Low overhead; Usually, a service business is the least expensive to go into as far as overhead. Although, now days you usually must be bonded with a very high bond and insured with a very high amount of liability insurance it keeps you from having to stock a lot of inventory and the office space you need is very limited to what you would need for a store with inventory. Of course, you will need the vehicle to go perform the service. But still the expense is exceedingly insignificant compared to the expense of opening a store or restaurant. You can even run a service business from your home.

Operate from anywhere; A service business can be run from anywhere, no one comes to the office it is all done over the phone, with you going out to the customers house. You can work the phones from anywhere. I have handled leads that come into my business when I have been in Florida with the phone forwarded to my phone, the people did not know where I was answering the phone from and did not care. I would talk to the customer, set up an appointment, call one of my employees and send him out. It is easy to run a service business from anywhere. Now with the Internet it is easier than ever. You can run a dozen different service businesses in a dozen different states from one location if you have people in the area to do the work.

Higher profit margin; You will certainly make more profit in a service business than any other. Because you are mostly charging for your expertise and time, not product. You may only spend a hundred dollars on product to do a thousand-dollar job.

Able to operate debt free; It is easy to run a service business debt free. You can have your workers on commission whether they are salespeople or service people, this will keep you from going into debt because of payroll. About the only thing you would need to finance would be your service vehicles.

No return merchandise; In a service business you do not have to worry about returns because of product defect or damage. In retail you always have a percentage of returns.

No break-ins stealing merchandise or shoplifters; When you are in retail, your biggest loss is from stealing, you do not have that in a service business.

The location does not hinder; Because you can operate from anywhere the location does not bother your business it is all by phone.

Do not allow fear to keep you from running your business properly.

Fear of failure will be your biggest threat to getting your business up and running properly. Do not allow fear of your competitors get you to do things that will destroy your business.

Do not underprice your service; A lot of people going into business get the idea that if they are the cheapest, they will get all the business. Do not believe that for a minute. Only a few people will take you because you are the cheapest, and if you price yourself too cheap you will not be able to do your best work and that will destroy your business. People buy because they think you are going to do the best job for the price. You will lose some because of price but not enough to worry about, you would not get them anyway, also the people who pay the lowest price usually complain the most. When I was in business, I was not the cheapest, sometimes I was the highest. But I learned You can price a job for $500.00 and do ten jobs to make $5,000.00 but you can price a job &1,000.00 and you only need to do five jobs to make $5,000.00. So, you lose some because of price you will make more over the long run and do a lot less work.

Do not overprice your service just because you can; sometimes you will run upon opportunities that would allow you to abuse people if you choose too. There will be times when you know people will pay you what ever you ask. Do not take advantage of the situation and over charge. Do what is right, you will win in the end.

Do not be afraid of competition; Just because there are a lot of other businesses around you doing the same thing you are doing does not mean you will not make it. When I opened my first service business There was competition everywhere, it looked like I would have been a fool to start that business. But I knew that business and I knew the competition would not be a problem and if I worked hard, I could make a success of it.

Don't allow the competition to get you to use gimmickry; There are a lot of companies that use gimmicks to get people to contact their business, but any kind of gimmick is in my view a trick or dishonest practice. I could give you a dozen different gimmicks that could be used to lure people in, but when you look at what is involved in each one and the motive for doing them, they are all trickery and dishonest. Offering a discount in your advertisement to track your ads is fine if it is a legitimate discount and not a way to jack the price up first so you can discount it later. Gimmicks are a desperate act of dishonest people.

Do not bad mouth the competition; This is something you should never do. This just reveals whether you have integrity or not. Most businesspeople are honest trying to make a living for their families, just like you. If you want to be treated right by the competition, then treat them right. Even if they bad mouth you, do not return the favor, you be better than that.

Always strive to be better and better and learn more and more. A lot of businesses go under because the owners never want to improve or learn more. There is no end to learning in this life, and that means about what you are doing in business as well as other things. You will never reach perfection in this life, but we should strive for it.

Take pride in the way you and your vehicles look. Always dress presentable when you are working. When you go to someone's house have on clean pressed uniforms and make sure your truck is clean and well-kept with the company name and phone number in substantial size letters that look professional. The way you look will decide who will do business with you. You will lose a good amount of business just by how you look and how your vehicles look.

Make sure your equipment is in good working order. Nobody wants to do business with someone who has junk equipment. I remember having a person mow my yard one year just to help him out, but he kelp showing up with junk mowers that would not run, and he would have to work on them or take them to be worked on every time he came, so I fired him. He got upset and wanted to know why I fired him. So, I told him his equipment was junk and because of that he could not to the work.

Always treat the customer with the utmost respect. You will keep customers and get more customers from the ones you have if you treat them with the utmost respect, Use the words Mr., and Mrs., use the words, yes sir, and yes mam, no sir and no mam. Never use any foul language around a customer. You should never use that kind of language any time.

Never allow anyone to work for you who drinks or smokes on the job. I know a lot of you will have a problem with this, but if you are a smoker, quit. People do not want someone who stinks of smoke or alcohol in their house. Also, people who smoke will destroy your vehicles with smoke.

Other businesses I have owned.

Another one of the businesses I have had was selling a certain kind of merchandise that I would buy in bulk at auctions and resale it wholesale and retail. I also did most of my selling of this merchandise on line on the Internet. Because of the price I paid for the merchandise, I could make a good profit and I would only have to sell a very few of the items to replace my cost and then the rest was pure profit. Let me give you an example.

When you buy you may have to buy three hundred to a thousand of one item in a lot, but you may only pay one to two dollars apiece for the items. You could then easily sale them at wholesale for fifteen to twenty dollars apiece or retail for thirty to forty dollars apiece. So, your profit on something you paid two thousand dollars for would be about thirty-five thousand dollars. We were doing about thirty thousand dollars a month on the Internet, this was many years ago when the Internet was in its early days. One thing that made it good with the internet was that we could sell all over the world and that we did. We shipped all over the world.

The biggest problem with this business was how you had to get the merchandise. You first had to go view it and it may be a thousand miles away. Then you had to go to the auction and bid on it. Then you had to go pick it up within about ten days. I always had to rent trucks to get the stuff back. There was a lot of time involved and a lot of expense in travel expense and truck rental. But, compared to the profit it figured out to a very small expense compared to the profit. The reason I got out of this business was I got tired for all the travel and the accumulation of all the excess that you didn't sell. It seemed like I always had more left over, and the buildup was happening very fast and unless you have some place to store the stuff you just throw it away. I had I don't know how many storage buildings full, every place in my house, my basement garage, etc. and had to take truck loads to the dump. But the profit is so good you could throw most of it away and still make a good profit. It just seems like there is none missing, even after you have sold thousands of dollars' worth, there is more left than when you brought it in.

One example of a sell of a small item about the size of a billfold. I paid about five cents apiece for about five hundred of this item and I sold them for five to ten dollars apiece. So, I made from three to four thousand dollars for an item I paid twenty-five dollars for. And I sold everyone of them and could have sold thousands more. It also didn't take up a lot of space

This business is still available today for anyone who would want to pursue it. Today you can do it all over the internet. And can even have your merchandise shipped if you choose. You can buy it without looking at it but, I would never do that unless you are a very experienced person in this field. I would love to do some more of this but, I just don't have the time now, I used to love the challenge of this. This can be done with out hardly any money, but you need to talk to someone and learn the business well before you begin to pursue it. You will wind up loosing everything you have by buying things that do not sell although they may look good and be new. Some items that are brand new, you can buy a whole truck load for twenty dollars, but you can't sell them because it is one of those things that will not sell. And what are you going to do with a truck load. Take them to the dump is all you can do. So, if you are going to go into this business, pay someone to teach you the ins and outs of this business.

Another service business I begin

I begin another service business when I moved to Florida. I had intended on buying a business from a man who was selling his in south Florida, but when I got there he had already sold it to some one else. I thought we had a deal, I talked to him before I left, and we had planned to meet on a certain day to exchange money and business, but he didn't wait, and I had no signed agreement and was out. So, I decided to start another service business, not the same kind I sold. We bought the equipment and started out to do business. Because of my sales experience and my experience of running other businesses it was no problem for me to get it going. I just went back to the basics of door to door sales. We did good in the business. So good I moved my oldest son and his family down to Florida to help us. My youngest son and I were already doing the business by ourselves. I first begin flying my oldest son down on Monday morning and he would work through Friday and I would fly him back home to Tennessee on Friday evening. It was a problem for him being away from his family so much that we moved him down and paid all his living expenses while he lived there. So, here was another business that begin making a profit right off the bat. And continued to make a profit and continued to grow with some large contracts until

I had to move back to Tennessee. Then we sold our contracts to another company.

This service business had very low overhead, even much lower than the business I had sold in Tennessee before moving to Florida, but it did not have as good a resale value. The business was simple and didn't need any special state license like the business I had sold. So, we begin making money right off. One thing you need if you are going to get a service business going fast, is someone with sales ability. This is the engine that gets the business started and keeps it going. I would recommend if you are going to start a service business and need to make a profit fast you need sales experience or willing to learn sales, or someone with you that can. It is possible to get a service business going through advertising. But it is going to take time and money to get ads working for you. A good source of leads will come from your existing customers, if you will ask for referrals from everyone you service, and work around the houses while you are servicing them, offering a discount to do theirs while you are in the neighborhood. You can also get other work from your customers by finding out if they have more work they need done. Some folks will have more than one house. Getting contracts on whole communities is a very good way to get business, especially in Florida. We worked with this kind of contracts most of the time, communities, condominiums and homeowner's associations. Those contracts run into the tens of thousands of dollars.

There is all kind of money to be made by those who are willing to do what it takes and are not afraid to try. Let me give you one warning about starting a business. Start businesses that you can start without going into debt. Keep your business debt free. My first business I started debt free and kelp it debt free all the way through the time I owned it. When I sold it, it was clear profit? Although after I sold my business I had the money to buy a business or invest a lot of money into a business, but I chose not to. I have never went into debt to start a business and have kelp every business I have had debt free.

Don't get me wrong, there are times you may want to put a lot of money out to purchase a business that is doing well and you know it is going to keep making a profit, or another business like the one you are already in, a lot of people will buy other businesses like the one they own to build up their own business, don't be afraid to do that after checking the business records thoroughly, making sure there are no liens or lawsuits associated with it. If someone is wanting to sell their business find out why. I mean find out the real reason not just what they tell you. It could be a person like me. I had just gotten tired of running the business and wanted to move to

Florida. So, I sold my business the first day I advertised it to the first person who responded. What did that tell you? You must understand that the business I was in was in very much demand and you very seldom saw one for sale. When one come up for sale it would sale fast unless it was way overpriced. Another thing it told me about mine was that I had it priced way to low, about half of what it was worth. The person that bought it didn't even try to negotiate the price he said right off, I will pay you full price, he saw he was getting a bargain.

I was sick after I sold it knowing I had lost so much money, but that was my fault. I took the money and moved to Florida to begin a new venture. Now the excitement was flowing again because I was going to have to begin something new. I got a real estate license when I first moved to Florida. I thought I wanted to try that, but real estate was not my thing. It is too slow, and aggravating and you don't make anything near what you can with your own business. There are also too many federal and state laws you must deal with. And another thing, you are just one of a million agents in an area, as they fall over themselves trying to get the business.

I tried franchise

Franchising may be good for some people, but not me. I don't want to discourage you from going the way of franchise if you really want too after looking it over good and having a lawyer go over it with you as to what you have and what you don't have. I looked at numbers of franchises and did my research on each one. I even bought one just to try it out. I didn't like it and never wanted anything to do with franchises again. The reason I would not buy a franchise is for the following reasons.

Most franchises are expensive to get into. Some of them will not even accept your application unless you have at lest a million dollars liquid to put up. Of course, these are the ones that do make money.

Everything must be done as instructed by the company. The company dictates to you every little thing. You can not weaver from that at all.

You have no freedom. You cannot even close when you want too. You must make sure the business is running according to the instructions of the company even if you must be there day and night.

You must pay a royalty out of ever penny you take in. There is never a time that you are through paying.

You really do not own a business, you only run a business for the company. You are like a manager of any other company out there but with more responsibility and work.

You cannot sell your business to anyone you like, but only who the company allows.

The home company rakes in the profits and allows you to do the work.

I cannot have a franchise because I need to be independent and be able to have full control over my business. In a franchise you have no control. If you feel comfortable running a business for someone else and paying them millions of dollars to let you run their business, then go with a franchise, but it is not for me. I don't want to report to anyone but myself and my Lord.

I hated every minute I was involved with a franchise because it was just like going back to work for someone else again and that is what I wanted out of when I left the work force to become my own boss. You will never regret starting your own business if you are a true entrepreneur, there is nothing like it in the world.

Some things that make it worth your while to start your own business.

You are your own boss. There is nothing like working for yourself. You are responsible to keep yourself motivated, without it you will get lazy. If you are a person that is working for an employer and you can't get to work on time, you must be continuously told to get to work, you always want to go on break and take longer brakes than allowed. You will never make it in business for yourself. You must have something that keeps you motivated if you build a business. There are things that will motivate you if you are a person that can be motivated. One of them should be that you do not have to answer to anyone but yourself. Your family should be a motivator as you think about how much more time you will have to spend with them and how much more money you will have to spend on them.

You have much more freedom. This is one of the things that I really enjoyed about having my own business. The freedom to do as you want when you want. You will have to wait until you have build your business to a certain point where you have employees to really be able to fully enjoy it, but you can even enjoy it without employees to a point by closing when you need too without asking anyone. When you have employees, you will be able to go as you please and leave them to run the business. This is one of the things my family and I took advantage of. I would get a desire to go somewhere for a few days and on the spur of a moment I would call my wife and tell her to pack some bags we are going to south Florida, or somewhere else for a few days. She would say when do you want to leave? I would say as soon as I can get home. I would run home pick up my family and we would leave. Sometimes we would be gone for three or four weeks. That is what you can do when you have your own business.

You make more money. This is true if your business is successful, but here we are not looking at a business that is not successful, I have been telling you all through this book how to do it and not fail, so we are not going to think that way. But the money you make with your own business is amazing. The first year I was in business for my self I made ten times what I made on the job I had before, and I was one of the best salesmen at that company. Do not make other people rich, while your family is struggling. If you can make the company you work for six figures a year, you can make that for yourself doing what you know how to do.

You are recognized in the community. When you are a businessman people view you from a different prospective. You get people's attention when you are a businessman. You get corporate discounts, your business card that gives your title as owner will get people to take notice. Let me give you an example.

My family and I went to stay in the Opryland Hotel in Nashville, TN. One night. The room was not up to my standards for the price I was paying. When I got home I called my secretary into my office and dictated a letter to the CEO of the company. I described the issue with the room in detail. I sent the letter using my company letterhead with my name as owner. In a few days I got a call from the secretary of the CEO of Opryland Hotel. I got on the phone with her and she transferred the call to the CEO. He was very apologetic and told me he wanted me to give him a date when we could come stay a weekend at the Hotel. I checked and gave him a date. A few days before the date his secretary called and said they were looking forward to our visit and when we got to the Hotel come to the special VIP section, don't go through the other check in and someone would be there to take care of us.

We arrived that day and the lines were backed up at the regular check in's We went to the door that said VIP opened it and walked in. You would have thought the president of the USA had walked in. They came over introduced themselves to us and when I told them my name they said, "Yes we know you and have been waiting for you." They offered us anything we wanted to drink and then had someone escort us to our accommodations. They never asked us for a credit card or any deposit or anything.

They took our bags and escorted us to one of the top suites in the hotel. The gentleman that was taking us to the suite said, I believe you will like this suite, it is one of a very few we reserve for only special VIPs, this suite is the most expensive we have in the Hotel.

 It was a marvelous experience. We have never been treated like that in our life. Anything we wanted we got. The room steward was checking all time to see if we needed anything. We stayed that weekend, checked out through the VIP checkout and did not receive a bill for one penny. Always go to the top when you complain and use the leverage you have as a business owner.

It also makes you feel like a different person. You are just able to feel good about yourself. You feel like you are not a failure anymore. Now you can go anywhere and feel comfortable that you fit in with the best of them.

You can deduct a lot of things as business expense. Now do not get me wrong, I am not saying that you can cheat the government by using deductions because you are in business that are not legitimate deductions. I am saying that because you are in business you will have a lot of legitimate deductions and make sure you use everyone you can.

Some things that are not good about owning your own business.

Self-employment tax. When you work for someone else, they hold out social security, but you only pay half, the employer pays the other half. Which is about 7.65 percent each. When you are self-employed you must pay both sides, which is about 15.3 percent, and this is off gross profits. That is why you need to deposit this tax each quarter. Because if you wait till tax time to pay you usually have a large tax bill.

Half of your employees Social Security tax. This is, yours to pay as well and this must be deposited each quarter. This can get expensive, but you need employees, but there is a price to pay beyond their salary.

Workman's comp insurance for employees. This is something that you must have on your employees, and it can get expensive.

Employees unemployment insurance. This is something you must pay as well in case you have to lay a worker off, he can draw unemployment. The premiums are not too bad at first only about two percent, until you have someone draw against you and then your premiums will go up to about ten percent. And that can be a lot when you have a large payroll.

Liability E/O Insurance. This is a requirement if you have most any business. And sometimes it can be expensive. This insurance is priced according to gross receipts with a minimum. If you have a new business you have no idea what you will gross for the year, so they will charge you the minimum. But, do not let that fool you. At the end of the year, you are audited, and then you must pay the increase in premium for what you went over, and it could be a lot. If the minimum is fifty thousand dollars and you pay the premium for fifty thousand then at the end of the year when the audit is finished, you have made two hundred thousand dollars. You then must pay the extra premium on one hundred fifty thousand dollars of receipts plus your premium for two hundred thousand dollars of receipts for the up coming year. This is something you must be careful buying, do not estimate too low the first year. Also, the state, usually has a minimum coverage you must carry according to the type business you have. It can be from one hundred thousand to millions of dollars coverage.

Surety Bonds. This is something all states require you to have, especially if you are working in people's house. The surety bond you must carry can be from thousands to millions of dollars according to the kind of business you have. A bond is not insurance although it works like insurance, but it is in case something is stolen or damaged in people's house. The thing about the surety bond is, it will pay out for you, but you must pay the money back, with insurance you do not.

Commercial auto insurance. This is the kind of insurance you must have on your service vehicles; it too can be expensive. Only hire people with a clean driving record. I do not know how many I have had work for me who wrecked my vehicles by just being careless.

Commercial license plates. This is just another way to get all the money they can from you because you are in business, but the commercial plates are more expensive than regular.

Income tax. The income tax that you pay will be according to your personal income, this will not change whether you are self-employed or not. It will be based on the net profit from your business after you fill out your schedule C Which is your business expense statement. You may also get some tax credit by buying a certain kind of vehicle

Do not look at all this expense and let it cause you to back out from starting a business. This is something everyone must face when starting a business. It looks bad, but it is not as bad as it looks because you will be making enough money to cover this expense and then have a good profit left over. Just be confident and move forward. Remember I did it without any money and so can you.

Remember you are never going to get there until you start.

Some things to stay away from.

Multilevel marketing. I know I will have a whole host of people who are going to get angry with me about this. Guess what? I do not give a rat's behind. Because I am not here to tell you anything but the truth, and for every- one person who has made some money from multilevel marketing you can fine ten thousand who lost their money and a lot of time. Also, with multilevel marketing comes the pyramid schemes that are illegal. There are many of these going and about everyone you know has either been in one or know someone who has, but you will never see anyone of them that has made any money in it. Stay away, you will thank me later.

Get rich quick schemes. Anytime someone tells you that you can make all kinds of money, without working, or just working one hour a day, and you can start making it fast, get away from that person. He is fixing to rip you off by selling you a package or program for doing what he said. If the programs they are selling would do what they say it would do, why are they selling it, why not just make the money themselves and keep the competition down? There are ten thousand of these programs out there and it grows every-day, and nobody makes money off it.

Post office worker jobs. These jobs do not exist, these are people trying to sell you information that is not beneficial at all, it is a waste of time and money.

About anything offered online. The internet is full of money-making ideas, so do not jump at these. About every one of them is nothing more than a way to rob you. Do not go online to fine out how to make money from anything offered there.

Anything that you must buy a kit for. This is a sales pitch to get you to buy a worthless kit. There will be no job or money to be made from anything in the kit.

Seminars for making money in real estate.
What you are going to get when you get in with
these people is a continuous paying out for more
information and training. You will be paying out
thousands of dollars before you are through and
never buy a property. What you need to do if you
want to start buying real estate, which is one of
the best investments you could have is get a real
estate license, get with a good real estate
company and learn all you can about buying real
estate. You will be able to learn all the financing
planes available, have access to all the real estate
that is on the market and you will be able to buy
real estate yourself.

Money making ideas sold on infomercials.
Many times, late at night you will see these
infomercials telling you how you can make money
fast and in enormous amounts with
extraordinarily little work. Someone will be telling
you how much he makes everyday while he
vacations in the Caribbean, or somewhere else.
He will show you what is supposed to be his fine
ten thousand square foot house on the beach and
his nice boat, expensive automobiles, etc. He has
a story that is very tempting. If you continue to
listen, he will have you believing all his crap, and
you cannot wait till he tells you how you can order
his money-making plan. He will have some CDs,
Workbooks, and a whole lot of material that he
wants to send you. He explains what each CD will

teach you and if you follow the plan you will be just like him in a truly brief time, making all kinds of money. WRONG! Look at the disclaimer in fine print that says, "There is no guarantee that you will make money with this". What they do not tell you is that the house, boat, cars and all the luxury items you saw were not even his, they were pictures he has of things he would like to have. Another thing they don't tell you is that after you buy his plan for the discount price of what was 1299.00 is now for this offer only discounted down to 199.00 because he does not want you to miss out on this great offer. If you buy this a few days after you receive it, you will get another call from them wanting to sell you an upgrade package that will get you going with a coach to help you. This package will be about a thousand dollars. Then a few days later if you buy that upgrade you will get a call for a better offer, this time you can even attend a conference that is only for a very select few that they have chosen to come. Those chosen are going to be taught by the man himself and you do not want to miss this. How much for this? Only five thousand dollars. It never stops, until you realize you have been had, and stop giving them any more money. If you happen to not be able to pay the thousand dollars on the first upgrade, they will discount it and let you make it in payments. If you can't afford the five-thousand-dollar conference, they will do the same, what they are doing is getting every dime they can off you any way they can, and you will never make a dime off the money-making plan.

There is no shortage of people wanting to rip you off, and there is no shortage of books, videos, recordings, courses, seminars and many other ways for them to get your money. I am not saying that there are no good books, recordings, seminars etc., but I am warning you that they are very few that will do anything for you but take your money. Remember a seminar is usually advertised as free, but the seminar is only a long informercial with a very pressured sales pitch to get you to buy the material they are selling. They almost tell you something in the seminar but stop short of giving you any real information because it will be in the package you have to purchase at the end, and they have different size packages for all those who have different amounts of money they can spend. Always remember this, **"anything that sounds to good to be true, usually is."**

Some of the con games and con artist of the past

There has been con artist all down through history and will continue to be if we live. Therefore, we need to always go into anything that we are looking at, where someone else is making us an offer with skepticism, because if you don't keep your guard up all the way through the presentation you will be sucked in. Let's look at some famous con artist.

Charles Ponzi Was an Italian con artist who lived from 1882-1949, Ponzi, got rich by promising investors fifty percent return on their investment in a truly brief time. What he was doing was taking the money from new investors and paying the older investors. This is the same thing Bernie Madoff was doing that sent him to jail. The phrase Ponzi scheme comes from Charles Ponzi's name. People still fall for this scheme today because of greed. When your heart and eyes get full of greed you are fixing to be taken.

Frank Abagnale Jr was known for his check fraud scheme that got him over two and a half million dollars in checks he cashed in every state in the union and twenty-six foreign countries before he was twenty-one years old. He is the one the movie "Catch Me if You Can", was made for. He was also a confidence man, an imposter of Doctors, Pilots, Attorney, and professor of a collage between the age of fifteen and twenty-one. He is now a very respected check fraud expert.

James Frey authored a book about his life of crime and addiction. The book became a best seller with him appearing on many talk shows. He was even able to take Opry Winfree in and made millions. But what was discovered later is that everything in the book was a lie.

The Fox sisters were three sisters from New York who played an important role in the creation of Spiritualism: Leah (1831–1890), Margaret (also called Maggie) (1833–1893) and Kate (also called Catherine) Fox (1837–1892). They fooled their parents, the community, and later the entire world by saying they could communicate with the dead through pecks and knocks. They made a lot of money with their con game but later died in poverty.

Victor Lustig (1890 - 1947) was a famous con man (who even conned Al Capone out of some money), but his most famous grift was "selling" the Eiffel Tower for scrap metal. When he read about the condition of the Tower at the time in the newspaper, he sent letters to a bunch of metal dealers posing as a Government official looking to sell the tower for scrap. Then he took a train to Vienna with a suitcase full of cash.

George Parker (1870 - 1936) kind of out-did Lustig, even though he came first. He "sold" a variety of New York City landmarks to unsuspecting tourists, including the original Madison Square Garden, the Metropolitan Museum of Art, Grant's Tomb, the Statue of

Liberty, and most famously, The Brooklyn Bridge, which he sold twice a week for years.

Lori Stilley a woman from New Jersey pretended to have stage IV bladder cancer, fooled her family, friends, and a host of other people for two years racking in thousands in donations from family and friends for treatment. I have seen this happen here in the town that I live in just this past year.

People have had the same problem from the beginning. They want something without working for it, and they are susceptible to being taken advantage of because of the greed in them. Whether you want to admit it or not People are lazy and greedy, but they are not without desires. Why do people fall for the health and wealth televangelist? Because of two reasons. One, desperation, many people are in a desperate situation and are looking for a way out. They can't pay their house payment, the electric bill etc. Many have health problems and are looking for a way out. Because of their situation and the offer from the televangelist of receiving a miracle if they will give a gift to the ministry, they take money they don't have to give and send it to the charlatan that is already rich and getting richer off desperate people. This group of people are the ones that really get my blood boiling when I think about them being abused by those racketeers and con artist. There is a special place in Hell for these people. Second, there is a group of people who respond to the televangelist out of greed. I don't feel sorry for those, because they are the same as the televangelist and deserve each other. This group hear them telling them that if they will give their money they will receive a hundred-fold in return, and they send the money just like a gambler plays a slot machine, hoping to get rich.

The televangelists are the worst of all the con artist because they use God to con people out of their money. They twist the scripture passages to make them say what they want them to say. They take scripture out of it's rightful context and try to build a doctrine on a lie. Anytime you change the scripture, reinterpret scripture, or just simply deny scripture, you are a heretic and not a true minister. **2 Peter 2:1-3 King James Version (KJV)** gives us some details about these preachers.

1 But there were false prophets also among the people, even as there shall be false teachers among you, who privily shall bring in damnable heresies, even denying the Lord that bought them, and bring upon themselves swift destruction.

2 And many shall follow their pernicious ways; by reason of whom the way of truth shall be evil spoken of.

3 And through covetousness shall they with feigned words make merchandise of you: whose judgment now of a long time lingered not, and their damnation slumbered not.

What Paul is telling us here is That these men are false teachers. They bring in their own teaching, not God's. and secretly slip in into the true doctrine so you will not detect it. They will even go so far as to deny the Lord ruling over them as they claim to be of God, but their works deny that they are of God. It is not just in what you say but, what you do, how you live that reveals whether Jesus is your Lord or not. They are heading for destruction and it is going to be swift. Many people will follow them and their destructive ways because many people love the way they live in denying the Lord's rule over them. I was telling you about those who are like them because of their greed. This is that group.

They act out of covetousness which is their love of money. That is what drives them. All they talk about is money. You will never hear the Gospel from them, everything they talk about relates to money. They use twisted words to exploit you.

Whatever they must do to a passage of scripture to get you to respond by giving your money they will do. Those people are headed to Hell, do not follow them. We also have the scripture in 1 Timothy 6:5 tells us of a group of people who are corrupt that teach a heresy that "Gain is godliness" saying that if you are a godly person you will receive a lot of wealth in this life. But Paul also goes on to say in verse 10 **that the love of money is the root of all evil.** Therefore, I said in the beginning do not pursue success because of money or don't allow money to be your number one motiving factor, because if it is you will be loving money and you will abuse people to get it. Money is a tool, use it like a tool and it will be beneficial to you, but if it becomes your god, that you worship, you will go down like all the other Bernie Madoff's out there.

Let me before I close this book tell you a little more about myself and the businesses I have been in. Although I had several businesses that were independently owned by me. I did at the same time have some additional businesses that I ran out of the same office because it was so easy to do. I could use my same office people to work all of them. I had an insurance license and was an independent insurance agent, that sold health and life insurance. I have had real estate license that I could also use to list and sell real property. I have done internet sales of merchandise with mail order. Also, I have added on different service businesses that would be considered a whole different type business and used my same workers to do the work. What I am showing you now is that you have so many opportunities when you are an owner of an independent business. Now you don't want to stifle your main money maker trying to get other businesses going, but if they will fit and it don't affect the production of the others, go for it. I was very privileged to be able to have so many businesses under one operation. What you can do is make your business name an enterprise or some enterprises, you can work all of them under one umbrella. Of course, you need to keep separate the paperwork from each business because of special insurance that some businesses must have, bonds that some businesses must have, special license that some businesses must have. Also, some businesses require special records that must be kelp. Let's look at some service businesses that are easy to begin and can be run together with out any problem.

Carpet cleaning. This is a business that can grow big for you. There are several franchises out there but, build your own independent business. Find a place to get some experience, even if you must work for someone a little while. But this can be a money maker.

Pressure washing. This is a business that can be started alone or added on to the business you have. You might not believe there is money to be made in this but if you are in south Florida this is a big business.

Lawn service. This business is good almost anywhere now days, because hardly anyone mows their lawn anymore. You can start this on its own or add it to an existing business.

Commercial Janitorial service. This is a business that every business uses. It is easy to go into but stay away from the franchise. Build your own. Learn how to price the service. Some businesses have you service every day, others three times a week, and others once a week. There is good money to be made here. This service is mostly night work and will not interfere with your day work. I would not recommend doing restaurants if you do not have too. Then again you may like restaurants. Doctors offices, banks, real estates, big businesses that employee many office workers. All commercial business is your potential customer. You usually charge by the month and bill once a month.

Window washing. This will fit in with any of the other businesses well. Or if you like you can do it alone. It can become a large business if you get into commercial, they are done on a contract.

Painting. House painting is a very profitable business, but you need to learn how to do it right before you take any jobs. There is a lot of business for painters, but people are very particular about painting, so you do not want to mess up.

Small engine repair. This is a big business if you learn the trade and people know you do it. There are courses you can take to learn all about small engines. You do not realize the money to be made.

Landscaping. This is something worth learning, about everyone needs landscaping and the profit is amazing.

Home inspections. This is a big business in this day. Every house that sales will have a home inspection. There are schools that teach this course and once you engage in it you will be surprised at how much business you will have. There is hardly any overhead and for a couple of hours work you can make 300-400 dollars.

Delivery service. This is a needed service for people who need things delivered fast.

House watching. This is something that is big in South Florida. Many people only live there a few months a year or some even less and they need someone to go by their house every few days to check everything. You can have a large list of houses to watch in a short while, and you charge a monthly fee.

Advertising. There are a few ways you can work this. You can use your car for a rolling billboard. Put ads on your car and drive around town, the clients will pay you a fee, daily, weekly, or monthly. Another way to sell advertising is to make menus for restaurants and have businesses to advertise on them. The restaurant does not pay for the menu, you charge the businesses that advertise a fee according to the size ad they want. Take out menus work good for this.

Plant rentals for offices. Most offices have plants that really help set the atmosphere in the office. Those plants are usually rented. What you do is for a monthly fee on a year's contract. You charge according to the type and size plants they get. Your grantee your service so if a plant dies you will replace it. You also service the plants every few days by watering, pruning, fertilizing, debugging, etc. About every office is a potential customer.

Portable car wash. There are a lot of people who never have time to wash their car. With a portable car wash you can wash cars anywhere. When you go to a place where there are a lot of workers, you can get a substantial number of the cars at the same place. You will also be able to get fleets from companies that have many vehicles. Do not discard this idea easy.

Appliance repair. This is still a big business and easy to learn. Many people would rather get an appliance repaired than get a new one simply because they are attached to the old one. You will be covered up with business when people know you do this work.

There are so many more, I could set here and think of many more businesses you could start easy. But this is fifteen I just took off the top of my head. Also, you will notice all these businesses could be run together from one location. You will be surprised at how easy it is to find a way to make money today once you get started. I hope you will take to heart the things I have said it this book and put them to use and become successful. I am looking forward to hearing from you about how this book helped you in your business venture.